Who Will Take the Children?

Who Will Take the Children?

A New Custody Option for Divorcing Mothers—and Fathers

SUSAN MEYERS and JOAN LAKIN

The Bobbs-Merrill Company, Inc.
Indianapolis/New York

Published by The Bobbs-Merrill Co., Inc.
Indianapolis/New York

Manufactured in the United States of America

First Printing

Designed by Sheila Lynch

Library of Congress Cataloging in Publication Data

Meyers, Susan.
Who will take the children?

1. Absentee mothers. I. Lakin, Joan. II. Title.
HQ759.3.M49 1983 306.8'9 82-17847
ISBN 0-672-52739-1

for Joan's children

LISA AND GARRETT

for Susan's children

LISA AND JULIE

We would like to acknowledge all the women, men, and children whose stories made this book possible, and thank the many friends who helped in various ways on the project.

Our gratitude goes to: Pauline Dilatusch, Cynthia Dilatusch, Philip Meyers, Lucille Meyers, Phil Meyers Jr., Lynne Gordon, Harold Feinstein, Jeremy Zwelling, Ilana Rubenfeld, Brewster Beach, Jim Barcaleone, Bernard Clair, Dr. Mary Cunningham, Ingrid May, Swami Prananda and Shahabadin.

Contents

Foreword

Both of us have young children who are living with their fathers rather than with us. Neither of us was judged unfit by a court. We did not "forsake" our children. We are involved and loving mothers who decided at the time of our divorces, and in concert with our former husbands, that the best place for the children was with their fathers.

Both of us are also psychotherapists. Our own experience and our work with others have convinced us that perhaps the most complex and distressing decision a mother can ever confront is that of choosing to live apart from her children. It is certainly one of the most misunderstood and one of the loneliest.

Neither of us, at the time we separately decided on this course, knew any other woman who had made such a choice. We were completely without models or guidelines. When we met each other, long after our decisions were made, and shared our common experience, it was the first time we'd ever talked about it to anyone else who really understood. The sense of relief and reassurance was enormous, even though the events were in the past.

What would it have been like, we wondered, if we had had the opportunity for this kind of sharing and support while we were in the midst of struggling over what to do? Recognizing that it would have been extremely helpful led us to begin conducting therapy groups for women who were living apart from their children or considering doing so. Out of the workshops grew ongoing support groups. Out of all of it came this book.

The material here is drawn from our own experiences as well as from those we have encountered in the workshops, the support groups, and the scores of personal interviews we have conducted over the course of the past year.

By sharing these experiences, we hope to alleviate the sense of isolation and guilt so many women suffer as they contemplate living apart from their children, the feelings of apprehension and inadequacy so many men experience as they consider taking on the caretaking role. We also hope to show that the custody option we're exploring can be a reasonable choice for a mother, an enriching one for the father. Other women and men have already traveled this formidable path and can serve as guides. The sound of their voices fills the pages that follow, and we thank them all for speaking up.

SUSAN MEYERS
JOAN LAKIN
New York City
April, 1983

Who Will Take the Children?

ONE

Our Stories

The first experiences we present in this book are our own. Both of us debated whether it was really necessary to include them. Since our stories would not be told anonymously, like those of the other parents in the book, we worried how people we knew might react to reading them. Did we have to make our own experiences public to be valid spokeswomen on this subject? Wasn't it enough that we were the professionals in this venture? We thought that if we didn't tell what had happened to us, we would just be contributing to the silence on the subject. And there has been enough silence. So our own stories follow.

Susan Meyers

The decision to have my children live with their father was the most agonizing I'd ever made. I made it painstakingly, examining the situation from all angles, scrutinizing my own motives, pondering the possible results. It took me a few terribly difficult months to arrive at it, with help along the way from professionals, friends, and from my soon-to-be-ex-husband. The course seemed the best one for all of us: for me, for my husband, and for our two daughters. I believe time has proved that to be true. Even so, the decision left me with the guilt and distress almost invariably experienced by women who make this choice. Even when we do it "right," so to speak, the price is high.

I couldn't have predicted that I would one day find myself living without my children. The idea would have been unthinkable. Early in my marriage, I resolved to be a perfect mother. To me that meant being there, being available when our children needed me, something I felt I'd sometimes missed with my own mother. And for ten years I was a full-time mother. I was thrilled by the births of my children. They seemed miraculous to me. I loved nursing and caring for them as infants, and I was engrossed in each phase of their development. I delighted in sharing their activities.

On paper, my marriage not only looked good, it looked like the American dream. Very much in love, we married in the early sixties. And in a few short years we had all the things we were supposed to want: two children we adored, a beautiful home in a New York suburb, financial security as a result of my husband's affiliation with a good law firm. I even liked my in-laws, who were lovely people and lived just a few blocks away. However, shortly after the birth of our second child, I realized that, despite this cornucopia of riches, I felt rather empty and depressed. There must be something wrong with me, I thought, and I'd better straighten it out. I entered therapy in 1968.

The next several years were, for me, a time of expansion and exploration. I returned to school to earn the degree I'd abandoned at the time of my marriage. I became involved in the women's movement, starting one of the first consciousness-raising groups in the area, lobbying for abortion reform, speaking and marching whenever a speaker was needed or a march was held. I then moved on to an examination of spiritual disciplines, studying and eventually teaching yoga, and practicing meditation. As I moved further and further away from the suburban mind-set, I began to feel more and more trapped by my environment. It was evident to me that I no longer fit into the life we had fashioned.

My husband was interested in my journey, and at many points along the way I hoped he would join me. I still wanted to change my life without leaving my marriage. But he was much more conservative than I. I had fantasies of our moving to some place like Colorado or California, atmospheres more in harmony with my new identity. He was firmly rooted to home and job. The conflict seemed unsolvable. But even though I was feeling dissatisfied and restless, I didn't think of leaving. I was obedient to my upbringing. I knew you stayed together for the children. It seemed to me that's what my parents had done.

In 1976 my husband came home one night and asked me for a divorce. He would like to remain in the house with the children, he said. I could be free to pursue my interests. I remember that as he broached this possibility I felt excitement, a sense of what that sort of emancipation could mean to me. It didn't last long. Quickly, that small flame of exhilaration was doused in a flood of questions: wouldn't my children feel I was deserting them? Who would be there when they came home from school? Who would drive them places in the afternoons? What would other people think of me? What would I think of myself? I felt plagued by these and other such questions over the next few months.

Several things aided me in this struggle to decide. One was talking with my husband. "Look at the difference in our personalities," he'd say. "You're the adventurer and I'm the homebody. You've been saying you want the freedom to do all these things. I'm interested in getting married again sometime, staying home evenings and weekends. Based on who we are, I think it's more realistic that I should have the kids. I think you'd be miserable as a single parent." Also of help were the sessions we had with two child psychiatrists who agreed that the important criteria in choosing the full-time parent was not sex but personality and desire: Who really wants the job and will be competent and committed? Who will really enjoy it most? We also met a few times with a family therapist. And there, as well as in my private therapy, I tried to gain some insight into what it was I really wanted. I also followed the suggestion of a friend that I make a list of the pros and cons of each possible choice. I prayed for guidance. I meditated. I even contacted an organization called Silent Unity, whose members pray twenty-four hours a day, and asked them to add my problem to their prayers. Gradually, out of my confusion and pain, things began to come into focus.

My daughters were ten and eight years old. I knew I didn't want to uproot them from their neighborhood, their school, and their friends to take them with me to New York City. Yet I had decided that would be the best place for me to return to school and begin a career. But I didn't know for certain if I'd like the city and stay there permanently. It didn't seem fair, under those circumstances, to yank my kids out of their familiar and comfortable environment. The other possibility was to stay in the suburbs nearer the children and commute to the city to school. But I hadn't even liked the suburban atmosphere when I was married. Wouldn't it be anathema to me as a single person? And what if I stayed in this environment I found so disagreeable just for the sake of my children? Would I end up resenting them and thus defeat the whole purpose of my being nearby?

Going over and over the pros and cons of each possible course sharpened my sense of my own needs and desires. I wanted to go to the city alone and begin to make an independent life for myself. I didn't want to "get away" from my children. On the contrary, I intended to make certain that I maintained my place in their lives. But I did want a chance to experience fully the freedom toward which I'd been moving for several years. I worried about the effect this would have on my children, but I knew that they would be well taken care of. I had no doubt that their father loved them very much and would be an excellent full-time parent.

So those were the factors, and finally I made my decision. I told my lawyer I wanted a joint-custody agreement stating that the children were to remain at home with their father, but that this "was in no way a reflection of the wife's fitness as a mother or of the depth of her love for the children." The agreement also stated that after the first year and at my written request, the place of residence of the children could be reconsidered and a decision made according to the best interests of the children; if my husband and I were unable to agree on what those best interests were, we would consult a mutually agreed-upon child psychiatrist to aid us in making the decision.

In making this choice, I'd sought objective opinions and searched my soul. The tension of going through this was so enormous that I'd gotten sick three times in a six-week period. But, making the decision didn't bring relief. If anything, the aftermath of moving out of the house was even more difficult. I was awash in regret and self-recrimination. I could think now only of all the good things that had existed in my marriage. I should have tried harder to make it work. And even if the marriage couldn't have been salvaged, I should never have left the children with their father. Children need their mothers. I should have stayed nearby, near enough to see them often and without the artificiality of a visitation schedule of twice each week and every other weekend. I shouldn't have chosen to live in the city. Hadn't I been too selfish? Had I considered my needs more than theirs? This must be a most unusual situation, I thought. The fact that I didn't know any other women who were living apart from their children proved it.

The responses I received from other people didn't do much to relieve me of these notions. While my decision wasn't greeted with the outright expressions of shock and hostility so many women encounter, I ran into a kind of sympathy that was almost as bad. "Oh, that must be terrible for you," people would murmur. "How awful, how difficult." I knew they assumed I'd "lost" my children, that they had been "taken" from me. And why would they assume this? Because they couldn't even imagine that someone would *choose* to leave her children behind. It would never enter their minds. This sort of sympathy spun me right back into my own guilt and questioning. Maybe I should have done this; maybe I should have done that. All the voices of my conditioning rose and taunted me. It was excruciating.

At the end of the first year, our deadline for reconsideration, my daughters expressed their wishes. They wanted to stay where they were; they did not want to move to the city. My ex-husband had remarried. They were ensconced in a new family unit. Visiting the house, where another woman was now living, was terribly painful for me. And at first, the fact that both of us existed was an embarrassment for my children, making them feel different, that most dreaded childhood affliction. They didn't know anyone else who appeared to have two mothers. My younger daughter used to ask that I not pick her up at friends' houses. This certainly indicated that she had feelings about her situation's being peculiar, and I tried to talk with both girls about that. More often than not they'd respond, "I don't want to talk about it." This made me feel terrible. How could I reassure them if they wouldn't express their feelings?

Now, six years later, all of us are comfortably used to this arrangement born in such torment and anguish. I think I made the right decision. It has worked out well for my daughters. They're healthy, reasonably happy children and, I imagine, not much different from what they'd be if I'd been living with them all along. It has worked out well for me. I've found the satisfaction and fulfillment I was seeking from an independent life and work to which I'm dedicated. I regret missing out on parts of my children's lives, the ordinary stuff of day-to-day living that can't be duplicated during weekends or holidays, which are "special" times by definition. Also, since the girls are now typical teenagers, their social lives are active, and they are less available for weekend visits. I realize this is a normal phase, but, as the visiting parent, I sometimes feel a loss of the contact we had in the early years when they both came to stay with me every other weekend. A full-time parent at least sees teenaged children as they run in and out of the house. But I feel that my connection with them is strong and that it will only grow stronger.

I love my children. I wanted them when they were born. I've taken pleasure and delight in them all their lives. I intended to be the best possible mother I could be, and that meant to me that their needs came first. For a time it worked. But then some of my own needs began to demand attention. Would I have been a better parent if I'd ignored those demands? I doubt it. Martyrs don't make good mothers; I'm quite sure of that.

Joan Lakin

I, too, was someone who had everything a woman is supposed to want. My husband and I lived in Paris in exceedingly comfortable surroundings: a beautiful house and lots of help. My life revolved around visits to galleries and fashion shows, lessons of every imaginable sort (cooking, riding, flying, languages), dinner parties that I prided myself on bringing off elegantly, and two children to whom I was devoted. Like Susan, I was determined to be a perfect mother.

For the first five years of my daughter's life I left her alone overnight only once, and then very reluctantly. Though I'd been working before she was born, I didn't return to work afterward because I coudn't find anyone I felt was sufficiently competent to care for her. I immersed myself in her, astonished by the intensity of my love as I sat for hours in an old family rocking chair, rocking her, singing and talking to her, nursing her on demand. I read to her long before she could understand language. I never left her alone for a moment. And the results seemed to vindicate my absorption: she was happy, healthy, outgoing, and developmentally advanced. It seemed that I was the perfect mother I'd set out to be. Now, looking back, I can remember a sensation I'd sometimes have when my daughter was asleep or wrapped up in play: a sudden great weight, arriving, I always felt, from somewhere outside of me, filling me with heaviness. Whenever this occurred, I rushed to distract myself from it and then did not think of it again until the next time.

By the time my son was born, seven years after my daughter, we'd been living in Paris for several years. Before his birth I'd been experiencing intimations of dissatisfaction, but when he arrived everything seemed wonderful once more. I gave myself over completely to motherhood. But this time it didn't shield me so effectively from those other parts of myself I'd been working hard to ignore. As delighted as I was with my son, I was also aware of an increasing sense of despondency. I entered therapy to try to discover what was wrong with me. Why should I be feeling this in the midst of my perfect life? I also joined an issue-oriented feminist organization and began attending a consciousness-raising group. As I gave my life closer scrutiny, I began to realize that what was missing from it was work that really interested me. Without that, my life felt wasteful and wasted.

Shortly after getting married I'd begun my master's degree in psychology but then set it aside to work full time while my husband attended law school. Each year we'd spent in Paris was supposed to be our last, so each year I'd planned to return to the U.S. to complete my degree and begin my doctorate. Then another promotion would come through for my husband, and I'd set aside my plans. Finally, I started to explore the possibilities of studying in Paris or London. Finding neither satisfactory, I began to think of returning to America to go to school.

As soon as I let myself entertain this idea, I was also forced to recognize something else I'd been protecting myself from seeing: my marriage was over. My husband had been my high-school sweetheart. I'd married him my last semester in college. My entire adult life had been governed by him, his schooling, his work, his career advancement. I had no idea who I was apart from him, but I knew that I wanted to find out.

The children and I returned to the United States, to New York City. The effect on all of us was jarring. I, who'd been used to full-time help and a life of leisure, was now completely on my own for the first time ever, in a city I'd never even visited and where I knew no one. In addition, I was attending school full time and had total responsibility for two children, one of them still in diapers. My husband, despite our separation, was quite generous financially, but, even without serious economic problems, the situation was uncomfortable.

Now my resolve was two-pronged: to excel in school and to be the best possible mother in these difficult conditions. My daughter was in school during the day; I paid someone to watch my son while I was in classes. When I was not in school I tried to give my son undivided attention, saving my studying until evening when he was asleep. I'd usually study from nine until one or two in the morning and then get up again with him at six. I was utterly exhausted all the time. Since the small amount of energy I did have went toward the boy, the youngest, the neediest, there wasn't much left over for my daughter. She and I weren't getting along, in any case. She was angry at me for leaving her father; angry that I'd yanked her out of the serene and sheltered existence she'd known and tossed her into a wholly different and disturbing environment; angry that I no longer had limitless time to devote to her, that I no longer seemed to be the same person she had known all her life. And, indeed, my disposition had suffered. I was nervous, pressured, worn out and given easily to flying into rages, behavior she'd never seen before. And, perhaps worst of all, throughout this period I was plagued by guilt every moment of every day because I felt I wasn't being a good mother.

After a year and a half, when their father suggested during a visit to New York that he take them back to Paris for a school term, it seemed a fine idea for many reasons. He was a good father who loved his children very much, and I felt certain he would be able to give them more genuine attention than I could. My daughter, I knew, given the acrimony that had developed between us, would prefer to be with her father. My son sometimes cried for him. For my part, the children's temporary absence would give me more time and energy to devote to finishing my degree. Nevertheless, even with all these positive aspects to the decision, it was awful when the children left.

I had been in therapy for the preceding year, but now I went every day for three weeks, trying to deal with the grief and guilt I felt, trying to work through my sense that the children would die without me, that I'd die without them. I used to imagine, during some of the many sleepless nights I spent, that I could hear them crying for me. The sense of loss I experienced was bodily, physiological. I felt as though the inner core of me had been ripped out. I don't think I could have survived without strong support from my therapist and a few close friends. They were the only people who didn't react to my decision with shock. I didn't know any other woman who'd made this choice; neither, apparently, did the people I was talking to. It was as unthinkable to them as it initially had been to me. I was so guilty, so distraught, that when people asked me about my situation, I would frequently either burst into tears or go absolutely stone cold and be unable to respond at all. I found myself, as time went on, often not mentioning that I even *had* children.

When my husband's work moved him to New York several months after this, he still wanted the children to reside with him. He was now living with the woman he would eventually marry; she loved the children, and they liked her. I was still in school and working as well and beginning to establish my practice as a psychotherapist. My daughter, though she knew she could live with me if she wished, chose not to. I believed it was important for my son to form a bond with his father. We could share taking my son to nursery school and picking him up. I would see him, and my daughter, several times a week, but they wouldn't have to live in the midst of the stress occasioned by my rigorous work and school schedules. I had worked through the worst of my nightmares about being without them. It seemed like a perfect solution.

At one point, before our divorce came through, my husband asked for full custody. Throughout our separation and during our conversations about where the children should live, I had always known that I wanted to avoid court at all costs. I didn't want to put the children through that additional ordeal, and court seemed a totally alien sphere to me, another planet, one whose language and customs I was ignorant of. The whole idea terrified me. Nevertheless, when he asked for full custody I said no and told him I was willing to go to court if necessary. He backed down, and we settled on joint custody, the children residing with their father.

This "perfect solution" was exactly that for a few years and then one day, with little warning, my ex-husband announced that he was moving to California. Our divorce decree stated that we were to live within two hundred miles of each other. I objected to his plans but finally was placated by the understanding that he woudn't be away longer than two years. I got nothing in writing, and I ultimately acquiesced in his decision, something I regard now as a very grave mistake.

During this new period of separation—three years ago now and with no end in sight—I have again experienced some of the guilt and grief and loss I felt the first time the children and I were apart. I miss them terribly. I miss them every day.

The basic decision to let my children reside with their father has yielded positive things for us all. For me, the time to complete school and establish my career, to make the transition from wife/mother to professional working woman, without the energy drain of single parenthood, was invaluable. I have no doubt that it was also good for my children to be spared the stress of my daily life while I was in transit. The move out of New York City was a settling, stabilizing one for my daughter, though the same effect could have been achieved if the move had been to Connecticut, not California. It's been good for her to live once again in a solid, relatively placid household with two adults. My son has also benefited from living in this environment, and it has been important for him, I believe, to have a male role model. My ex-husband has certainly delighted in having the kids with him.

Today my relationship with my children thrills me; there's no other word to use. But that didn't come easily . . . or quickly. It was an arduous, painful process to get to where we are today. All of us were angry. At one point I was angry that I even had to deal with the issue of children. I'd look around me and see other people getting on with their lives and careers without the anguish I was experiencing. Why me, why do I have to have children? I would lament. The answer was simple and certainly not the children's fault. I had been on track all my life to get married and have children. I was groomed, conditioned, trained to be a mother. Even being a wife was secondary, in a sense, just a crucial step along the road to motherhood. When I discovered that all my needs and desires could not be encompassed in that single role, the conflict of moving beyond it was awful. And it made me angry that I had to go through it. My children were angry at me, and rightly so, for turning their world upside down. Sometimes, when we were all living in New York, they didn't want to see me. My son would convey this rather obliquely. "I don't like all the plants in your apartment, Mommy," he'd say. "I don't want to come there because there are too many plants." My daughter was much more direct. She'd make appointments with me, then fail to appear. Bolstered by therapy, I just kept coming back and showing up and being there, without displaying any anger toward them. I was the initiator of this disruption, my therapist reminded me; it was my responsibility to be constant with my children no matter how they treated me. I'd had my time for anger; they deserved theirs. And no matter how hurtful it was, I owed them the time and the space to express it. That counsel served me well, paying off, as it has, in the rebuilt trust that exists between me and my children today.

I made lots of mistakes as I fumbled through this process of becoming a mother who lives apart from her children. There are many things I'd do differently if I were reliving it today. But my biggest regret is that I let my children move so far away. That kind of distance isn't good for anyone, for the children or for either parent. Time spent together on holidays and vacations is no substitute for constant, steady exposure to one another. All of us who live apart from our children relinquish sharing the ups and downs of their daily lives. Those of us who live very far away miss out on great pieces of our children's growing up, a unique time, a time that will never come again.

TWO

Myths and Assumptions

A mother who lives apart from her children, even in the enlightened eighties, is still an object of stereotypical surmise. Knowing just one fact about her—her living arrangements—we freely fill in the rest of the picture. She could only be without her children because a court of law found her an unfit mother or she simply didn't want her children and has given them up. In either case—whether her children were taken from her or abandoned by her—she's suspect. At best, she's probably a borderline type, somewhat defective; at worst, she might be a full-fledged monster.

One or More of the Above

We imagine the personality of such a mother. She's probably a cold sort, uncaring, unresponsive to others. She's certainly selfish: it's obvious that she has put her own interests before those of her children. She must be neglectful and irresponsible: no conscientious adult walks away from a child. Maybe she's a women's lib type who thinks asserting that it's *her time* to do *her thing* gives her license for aberrant behavior. Or perhaps the picture is tawdrier: she's promiscuous, subjecting her kids to a parade of strange men in and out the house. Or crazy: either a garden-variety neurotic who can't cope or a bona fide lunatic. Or could she be a junkie, a criminal perhaps? After all, aren't immorality, mental instability, drug addiction, alcoholism, or criminality really the only reasons why a mother doesn't have custody of her kids? Hasn't a husband always had to prove his wife was one or more of the above in order to gain custody himself?

Underlying all these assumptions is the central myth that governs attitudes toward mothers and custody: good mothers do not leave their children—*no matter what.* Our laws no longer support this myth. The maternal-preference rule, which became the custody guideline at the turn of the century and contained an automatic presumption in favor of the natural mother, has given way to "the best interests of the child" doctrine, which recognizes that either the mother or father is a perfectly suitable candidate for custodial parent. This doctrine is the sole criterion for determining custody in a majority of the states today. But people's attitudes, it seems, have not caught up with the spirit or the letter of the law. We continue to respond to mothers living apart from their children as if they were "unnatural." And is there anything worse that can be said about a mother? The reverberations of "unnatural" cover every negative possibility.

There have been, of course, recent and substantial parenting changes in our society. As noted, a new standard for determining custody has emerged. And, increasingly, parents facing custody decisions and judges who must rule when custody cases reach the courts are coming to believe that, in some instances, the father can serve a child's best interests just as surely and as competently as the mother can.

"Kramerization" is Well Established

Certainly, the custody deck is still stacked in favor of the natural mother. But, just as certainly, more men than ever are today seeking custody of their children. The 1980 census reported that more than one million children reside with their fathers under formal custody agreements—*an increase of 65 percent since 1970.* Many more children reside with a father who doesn't have the benefit of legal custody. A New York matrimonial lawyer reports that in the past year every father he's seen has at least very seriously explored the idea of a custody arrangement in his favor. Support groups for single fathers are burgeoning. The fathers' rights movement increases its membership. Studies are funded to analyze male parenting. Newspapers and magazines regularly carry articles proclaiming and exploring "the new fatherhood." The phenomenon dubbed "Kramerization," after the movie *Kramer vs. Kramer*, grows apace. What was formerly considered unspeakable—a mother without her children—is now at least being discussed, although in somewhat muted tones. Changes have taken place in our society in the last decade that have begun to make quavery the lines delineating the mother and father roles.

Undoubtedly, the force that did most to effect these changes was the women's movement, for it caused women in large numbers to question their assigned roles as wives and mothers. And that questioning became part of the erosion of sex-role stereotypes. Things were no longer as clear as they had been.

Wanting Out

I lived with the traditional view of motherhood during the ten years I was home with my kids. I accepted it, but at the same time I felt guilty about it. I didn't like to make cookies with them. I didn't like to sit endlessly and play games, in conversation with another adult I wasn't willing to be interrupted at their whim. Then a friend gave me The Feminine Mystique, *and I sat up all night reading it, often in tears. Someone was saying what I'd been feeling since I was six years old. I was raised to be compliant and dependent. Being successful meant giving up having love and a relationship. The women's movement was very important. It meant a lot to me.*

I always wanted to be what my husband wanted me to be. I grew up in a fairly matriarchal household, but it wasn't particularly happy, and I may have thought, based on that, that it's better if the man dominates the house. When we were first married he wanted me to be a mother to his children, just as his mother had been. I should be home all the time, have cookies and milk for the kids at three, things like that. But then he went out into the business world after graduating from college, which I put him through, and he'd come home admiring the professional women. So I was very confused. "What do you want?" I'd ask him. "Now you want me to go to work, now that I have the children?" But when I made attempts to work he was never very impressed with anything I did. I felt like the rules had been changed on me in midstream. I'd lost my independence when I got married. I'd lost my sense of what I wanted to do, and I had a very hard and confusing time until I found that again.

I was twenty when I got married to a man who was seventeen years older than I was. He'd been married before for fifteen years, but his ex-wife hadn't wanted children. So he was very eager to have kids right away, and we did, and he was totally devoted to them. He couldn't wait to get home from work to see them, he was so tickled with them. But the whole thing was very dissatisfying for me. I was about twenty-three or twenty-four when I started to think about leaving. I felt I wanted to get out in the world. Then I read Betty Friedan, and I knew I wanted to go to work. I wanted out.

Women began to explore hitherto neglected aspects of their lives. Full-time motherhood was not the only option. Some women returned to careers they had abandoned when they married or when their children were born. Others began, or returned to, educations that would lead to careers. And the world didn't end. Nor did their children appear to suffer egregious harm. Some women even maintained that their children benefited from it.

I think when I went back to graduate school, when I was on my own a little more, that I was a better mother. I think, for instance, that the attention I'd been paying to my daughter might have been of the suffocating variety. She really flourished and came out of herself after I went back to school. We both blossomed.

I'm very much a working person, and when I "settled down" after I got married, I wasn't fulfilled. I knew it was important for me to get back into the work world. If I'm living my life completely, I think

I'm bound to have more to give my kids. I know women who are locked in with their kids twenty-four hours a day, and it's awful. There's nothing positive going back and forth between them. What happens between me and my daughters, on the other hand, is very exciting.

I had what was considered an ideal life, I guess. In fact, there was a time when I *would have considered it ideal. I had a husband who loved me, two beautiful children, a lovely home, no financial worries, lots of help, and plenty of friends. But I didn't have any meaningful work, and that left a great gaping hole right in the middle of all that perfection. And the absence of work in my life began to make me more and more dissatisfied, and that dissatisfaction started to spill over onto my kids. It's impossible not to see them in some way as the force that's tying you down, and that adds up to resentment, and a resentful parent isn't a good one. Even with less time for my kids, I'm sure I'm a better parent working than not.*

Role Reversals

At the same time that women in some numbers began to recognize their need to work, their need to push at the confining boundaries of the wife/mother role, inflation became a seemingly immutable fact of life, and the number of women entering the work force grew even larger. Today, nearly 60 percent of women with children are working outside the home. And when women began to assert their freedom to move into new spheres, so did men. They began to see that perhaps full-time breadwinning wasn't *their* only role. They started to explore their nurturing, caretaking capabilities, which had been eclipsed in the past by a focus on work.

The questioning by both women *and* men of the roles they had been assigned by our culture has made us look anew at some hallowed assumptions. Are women, by virtue of the "maternal instinct," really better equipped than men to raise children? Is it true that men aren't as capable of nurturing as women are? Do children really need a mother more than a father? These old notions certainly haven't been blown to smithereens, but they have been shaken up.

We've begun to believe that both sexes might possess qualities formerly thought to be the attributes of only one. We've known for some time now that caring and tenderness are not exclusively feminine traits, any more than assertiveness and independence are solely masculine ones.

Letting Go—and Holding On

One result of all these changes is that today some divorced women are *choosing* to live apart from their children. They have not been judged unfit by a court. They have not run away from their children, "deserting" or "abandoning" them. What they have done is to see that there is an option for a father to raise his children, and they have chosen to exercise that option. They have not "given away" their children—nor the love, caring, and involvement they have for those children. The only thing they have really let go of is the role of full-time, or custodial, parent.

We should make clear at this juncture that we will not always be discussing legal custody agreements when we talk about women who live apart from their children. Our concern is where the children live and who fills the roles of full-time and part-time parent, no matter what the terms of a formal custody arrangement may be. It is true that some of the women we interviewed had given up custody altogether, legally designating their children's father as the custodial parent. Others shared joint custody with their ex-husbands, but the children resided with the father. (There are two kinds of joint custody: legal joint custody, wherein the parents share the rights and responsibilities of child rearing; and physical joint custody, the much rarer sort, wherein the parents share equal living time with their children.) In still other instances, however, the mother retained custody even though the children no longer resided with her.

Parents frequently neglect to change the formal custody designation out of a simple desire to avoid any legal entanglement. In other cases, the reasons for letting the custody designation stand are more complex and, in the main, symbolic. Some women who aren't entirely comfortable with the decision to let their children reside with their father may hang onto formal custody as a kind of security blanket. It says to them that the arrangement is temporary, that they could take their children back at any time. It says they aren't really separated from their children. Some women retain formal custody just because they can't bear the feeling of losing one more thing. Divorcing is, in itself, a time filled with feelings of loss and separation, and a woman may seize gratefully upon any way to minimize those feelings.

Not long after the divorce, I let the kids go live with their father. I sold the house in the suburbs and moved into an apartment in the city, which was a completely strange environment for me. Almost as soon as I arrived, my best friend got a job and moved to Milwaukee. The man I was dating moved to Florida. I felt totally abandoned. I couldn't sign over custody to my husband though because I felt I'd already given too much away. I knew it would take too much out of me to sign that piece of paper. He just had to accept that I wasn't going to ask for the kids back. I couldn't sign it. So legally they're still in my custody.

Part-time Parenting

To state that a woman has given up the role of full-time mother doesn't sound so earthshattering, does it? In the context of the changes that have occurred in our society during the last fifteen to twenty years, it sometimes seems almost logical, a patently reasonable alternative, for a woman to assume the role of part-time parent for a period of time.

For the next ten years my husband and I have arranged that I will be the visiting parent and he will be the custodial parent. He's about to remarry, and I like his new wife very much. He lives in the city where the kids have been living, and I'm going to be living in the country, which would mean they'd have to go into a new school system if they came with me. Also, I'm going to be getting my broker's license and getting involved in real estate, which will take me out of the house in the evenings and on weekends—exactly when the children would be home. I'm certainly going to visit the kids as much as I can in my free time, but I believe my husband would be better suited to be the custodial parent for the next ten years. After that we'll enter into a more equal time-sharing arrangement.

A High Price to Pay

That account sounds neither inflammatory nor revolutionary. Cultural changes have made it possible for a woman, in all good conscience, to not want custody of her children. Apparently, however, the changes haven't gone deep enough, for we continue to make mothers living apart from their children pay a high price for the choice they have made.

Look at the telling language with which we describe these women and their situations. In the late sixties and early seventies, when this phenomenon first began to receive attention, they were called "runaway mothers." In actuality, few of them just fled their homes without warning, severing all contact with their children. Yet what else does the phrase runaway mothers suggest? We talk about the children of these women as "abandoned" and "deserted."

I really felt people looked on me as some sort of freak. I mean, this is simply not something that any normal *mother does, right? And other people weren't the only ones who thought it was peculiar. I bought it, too. What kind of mothers don't have custody of their children? I asked myself: drug addicts, prostitutes, crazies, and criminals.*

An Attitude Frozen in the Past

But contrary to what our pejorative labels imply, these children are being raised by their fathers, blood relatives, after all, and being given, in most cases, the same quality of care they would have received from their mothers; in some cases, care of a superior quality. We say these women have "given up" their children. The truth is that most of them remain actively involved with their children and involved in an attentive and loving way. Generally speaking, a visiting or part-time mother tends to stay more immersed in her children's lives than a visiting father.

The present climate of our culture is such that it's possible for a woman to choose to live apart from her children. But it's not possible for her to do so with impunity. Even as more and more women make this choice, cultural attitudes toward it seem to remain frozen in the past.

Listen to a women who in 1935 took the then virtually unheard-of step of leaving her son with his father.

> *I was married at eighteen to a man chosen by my mother, and starting the day after I was married, I left him at least once a week as long as I stayed with him, which was six years. He wasn't a bad man, but I just had no feeling for him, and that made our life together a nightmare for me. My son was born thirteen months after we were married. If I'd been independently wealthy, I'd have taken him and gone away. But I had no money, and I couldn't have stayed away from my husband in that town. It was a town of 2,500 in Tennessee, and a divorced woman there was just a step or so above a whore.*
>
> *Well, it only got worse, not better. But I stayed because of my son, working to try to save money. His grandparents cared for him while I worked. I was like a mouse in a cage, going here and there, and I just wanted to get out, just out.*
>
> *When I met my second husband and fell in love with him, he begged me to go away with him. And I did. This was an opportunity to be with a man I loved very much, and I felt I could take a chance on myself. But there was no way I'd take a chance on my son, on hurting him. I didn't know how this was going to work out. I wasn't sure I could trust this man. And I knew my son was safe where he was, that he was well taken care of. I felt he'd be okay until I could take him with me. I believed this was only temporary. I'm not saying what I did was right, but it was something I was absolutely forced to do. Until you've been married to someone you do not love and have to touch him, you don't know what hell is. All you want is away, you want out.*

My family thought it was a horrible thing I'd done. My mother was almost hysterical, and my sister blamed me for ruining my mother's health. The worst thing you could say about any woman was that she'd left her children. In everybody's opinion, I went from being a very good girl to being a very bad girl. They were very, very critical. "It just isn't done," they'd say. "Nobody's ever done it. It's not fair to the child."

During this time I never discussed it with anyone. I made my decisions on my own. My first thought was my son; I didn't want to hurt him. But, if I'd had to stay there, I would have blown my brains out. So I had to leave. I tried to do what was best for everybody.

As it turned out I never did have my son come live with me. They all said I'd done enough harm by leaving his father. Why should I ruin his life too? There was an incredible amount of pressure. So I left him there. I could see he seemed content and happy. He'd grown up there; he had lots of friends, and his grandparents' lives revolved around him. But I was torn apart. I cried myself to sleep lots of times, thinking about my child. It isn't easy to part from a child after you have carried him for nine months and raised him. They're a part of you, like your right arm. You don't leave them easily. It's hard, but you try to think what's best for them.

I was scared to death inside. And when I cried, I cried alone. This is the first time I've ever told all this to anyone. But I think I did all I could do, all it was possible to do, in the only way possible to do it. I accomplished what I wanted to, and I didn't look back. My only regret was being apart from my son, but I was glad I had had him because he was a nice little boy, and I loved him very much.

We've talked about it, my son and I. It doesn't seem to have affected him. He laughs now and he says: 'I don't see how you put up with my dad as long as you did.' I think he respects me. We enjoy being together. I think he loves me and he knows I love him.

Unchanged: The Emotional Essence

Certainly there are aspects to this nearly fifty-year-old story that indicate how our culture has changed. The arranged marriage dates it, as does the idea that the only escape from a bad marriage is through another man. Divorce is easier today. Mobility is greater. The same woman in a similar situation today would most likely be able to escape on her own from that little Tennessee town. But there are also many elements in this tale that make it remarkably contemporary.

First of all, this mother's concern for her child was a prominent factor in the choices she made. She stayed in a nearly unendurable marriage for her son's sake, and when the time came for her to leave, she made what she felt was the best choice for him. She knew that he was well taken care of. She wasn't going to uproot him and carry him into unknown territory with her. She recognized that the solution was not ideal. But it did seem the best possible arrangement under the circumstances.

The shock and disbelief that her decision produced in her family are reactions that we heard expressed over and over again in our interviews. This woman could not have done anything worse as far as her family was concerned. Far from supporting her at this difficult time, they judged her severely. They were ashamed of what she had done and adopted a punitive attitude rather than a helpful or understanding one.

She went through this devastating experience entirely alone. She spoke to no one about her decision, and she kept her pain to herself. The sense of loss she felt at leaving her child behind was acute. But despite all the grief, all the anguish, she felt she had done the right thing, had found the best possible solution to a difficult problem. She still believes that now, and time, it seems, has proved her right. Apparently, her son did not suffer any irreparable harm, and today the two of them are able to maintain a loving relationship with each other.

The emotional essence of this woman's experience is nearly identical to that of many women who are taking this step in the eighties. Often, during our interviews, we heard these same feelings mirrored, sometimes almost word for word. And it is stunning to realize that not all that much has changed. the numbers have altered—many more women today are choosing not to reside with their children—but attitudes, for the most part, have not. Women who embark on this course now are doubly cursed, just as they always have been: they experience the sense of loss that comes with physical separation from their children, and they suffer as well from the shock and hostitlity that all too frequently greet their decision.

The Dictates of Conditioning

What are some of the reasons for this harsh disapproval? The laws in most states today affirm that a mother and father are on equal legal footing in terms of custody. They are to be considered equally suitable for the role of custodial parent. Despite this legal assertion, however, it seems that many women and men continue to harbor a maternal preference in their hearts and minds. Our conditioning dictates it. In some part of ourselves we continue to believe that women are somehow better at parenting than men are. We assume that women automatically know how to perform as parents. Men, on the other hand, must be taught such skills or come up with someone who can exercise them in their stead.

When a man is involved in a custody suit, he is often required to demonstrate that he can provide a substitute mother for his children in the person of a housekeeper, a prospective stepmother, a grandmother, etc. A working woman involved in a custody suit, however, a woman, in other words, who would be operating under the same time pressures as a man, is not asked to take the housekeeper pledge. We assume that a woman can do it all, by herself—manage a job, a house, her children—while a man needs help. And why do we assume this? Because a woman has a maternal instinct that allows her to perform any child-care work easily and naturally. She simply knows how to do so intuitively. Doesn't she?

In the last few years some women have made the audacious suggestion that no, she does not. They have let it be known in print and in their daily lives. The sacrosanct notion of the maternal instinct has been called into question. Among the scores of women we've talked with, the majority had strong maternal feelings and a sense of taking to motherhood quite naturally—but a significant minority did not. If we take the maternal instinct to mean a natural aptitude for, and interest in, the daily caretaking of children, our small sample of women was decidedly mixed.

Maternal Feelings: Natural or Not?

I gave my kids everything I possibly could when they were small, and I loved doing it. I took them everywhere with me. I had my hands on them all the time, giving them constant affection, constant touching. I always held them and talked to them. Those first few years were fabulous.

I never felt capable of being a mother. I was eighteen when I got pregnant because I didn't know how to use the diaphragm my mother had rushed me to get so I wouldn't get pregnant. I wouldn't even have thought then whether I wanted a child or was prepared to have one. My God, who ever heard of such a thing! As a woman who's quote normal unquote, if you get pregnant, you want the child. I gained 110 pounds with the first kid, and it was awful . . . not one of these pleasurable mother experiences . . . it was awful. It's funny but I have some film, and someone saw it and said she'd like to use it in a workshop she was giving. For what? I asked her. And she said, "to show people how not to handle a baby."

So I never felt capable. I never felt like I was a good mother. And then I really didn't care. I didn't have this undying love I was supposed to have for my children. I was scared of my first child. I was afraid that I might drop him or not feed him right or get the tub too hot. I was afraid of everything. It didn't make me feel good to be with my children. I never dressed them right, according to my mother, or never fed them right, according to my mother and my husband. Whatever I did was wrong.

It came very naturally to me to be a mother. I loved my children and loved being with them, especially when they were babies. I never had any feeling of resentment toward them, any feeling that they imposed limits on me.

My son hasn't lived with me since he was just about two years old, and I've always been very satisfied with our relationship. I haven't wanted him to live with me. But when he was about nine he started to make me feel very guilty, and I began to think he should live with me. Without telling him, I began to make plans, and I had everything arranged for him to move in. Then one day I went into a therapy session, and my therapist asked if this was what I wanted. Immediately I started to cry and said no, though I didn't know why. But I came to certain realizations, and since then I've come to accept that I am just not maternal. I never was. When I was thirty-five I had my tubes tied, and I felt great relief.

Even though I was unhappy with many aspects of my marriage, I was very satisfied with my role with my kids. I loved being a mother.

We don't always fit the roles we're assigned, you know. Sometimes we're round pegs in square holes. For me, a traditional marriage was a round peg in a square hole, and traditional mothering was the same.

I love my kids, and being their mother is one of the nicest jobs I'll ever have. I had a lot of fun with that, and I did a good job. They're sweet, dear people, and I really enjoyed being with them.

Because children come out of your body, it doesn't necessarily mean you're on the same wavelength. It doesn't necessarily mean you know what to do and feel what you should. That's a misconception. When my children were born, I remember feeling very dependent on my husband. He was a veterinarian, and I felt he'd had the experience of dealing with the process of birth and would know how to take care of everything. He was like my instructor, my mentor. He taught me how to make baby food from scratch so that it wasn't loaded with sugar and salt. He encouraged me to breast feed. I didn't enjoy it when my son nursed. I was totally exhausted and didn't like getting up in the night. In general, I didn't enjoy the pregnancy or the children when they were little.

I was so thrilled with my first child that I couldn't wait for him to wake up. I was really into the whole thing of being a mother. And I wanted another fairly soon so they could be companions. So I had another eighteen months later. They were both boys, and I really wanted to have a girl so we had another. We have three kids and I wanted them all.

I had very mixed feelings about motherhood. There were parts of it I enjoyed, but I also found it very difficult. It was draining, and I had moments of regretting it. As soon as it was possible for me to go back to work after my kids were born, I did. It wasn't that I had to. I wanted to.

I grew up playing house, playing dolls, and thinking it was wonderful, and my early years with my children were an extension of that. It seemed very natural to me, very easy. I was very loving with them. I gave them a lot of love and nurturing when they were infants.

I didn't know what I wanted, but I knew I wasn't happy being a wife and mother. I didn't place any value on it. Anybody could do this, I thought. I loved my son, but I was bored. I knew there had to be something else. For a time I was afraid to try other things, so I just had to bear with it. But I didn't want to bear with it. It really didn't suit me.

I was an absolutely devoted mother, probably overattentive. My children just thrilled me when they were born, and I loved spending time with them.

I don't think motherhood was all I thought it was supposed to be. It wasn't just pink booties. It was a lot of spit-up and dirty diapers, and I found that very irritating. If I'd known then what I know now, I wouldn't have had children at all. I think unless you've got a lot of money so that you can do for those children what you want, giving them dancing lessons, say, or putting meat on the table all seven days a week—unless you can provide for that child like you want to—I don't think you should have them. It shouldn't be so automatic, like well, I just got pregnant today, and we'll make do. You should really want it. I got pregnant with my youngest because everybody told me I shouldn't raise an only child, that I'd regret it, that I wasn't doing my oldest child any favor. But they didn't say that if I did that I would then be raising two children at the same time.

Automatic Assumptions

There is, obviously, a wide range of experience among women with regard to the "maternal instinct," or lack of it. However, most women contemplating a divorce automatically assume they will keep their children. This expectation is not necessarily based on desire. Nor does it always reflect an assessment of what's best for the children. It's just a given, and a very strong one. For it isn't only other people, the commenting chorus of society, who believe that a mother belongs with her children, no matter what. It's mothers as well.

> *My ex-husband and I were approaching a separation, and I had become increasingly conscious of problems I was having with motherhood. I spent a great deal of time thinking about both of these things, but it simply never occurred to me that I might have the option to live apart from my kids. That's just something a woman doesn't do.*
>
> *My feeling that a mother has to be with her children was so strong that I might never have let my kids go if their father hadn't just kept at me about it, year in and year out. I can see now that it's a better situation for me and a better one for them. But I could never have taken the initiative on it.*
>
> *When I let my kids live with their father I sort of rationalized myself into it. I told myself that it would just be for a while and we'd basically split them down the middle. Then it evolved that they lived with him more than with me. That kind of eased me into it because it was anathema to me.*

There are several reasons why not living with their children is such an unacceptable notion to so many women. First, as we've noted, there is the cultural conditioning that says *this just isn't done*. We have been taught that good mothers don't leave their children. If these mothers aren't living with the kids, they are considered to have left them. Sometimes this conditioning is so powerful that it prevents the option of not living with her children from entering a woman's consciousness. The notion never even gets on the list of possibilities. Second, there is the knowledge that going against this cultural conditioning can extract a heavy penalty. Just as there are women to whom the option of living apart from their children never occurs, so are there women who allow it to occur, who fantasize about it, but who would never dream of giving voice to those fantasies. They are fearful of even verbalizing such shameful ideas.

> *I remember thinking what it would be like to be without my children, the freedom I'd have, the time to myself. But I would never have said that out loud. I could barely let myself* think *it, and when I did, the guilt was awful.*

> *When both my children were very young I used to sort of daydream about being somewhere else. I used to wish that I lived all alone, no husband, no kids. I got married to get out of my family's house but I felt just as trapped with my husband as I used to be with my family. Of course I never told anyone. It was bad enough that I had these thoughts.*

Old Ideas Die Hard

These women keep their mouths shut because they're afraid of the name-calling. They don't want to be labeled "unnatural," "unfit." Until quite recently, the only way a man could gain custody of his children was by proving that his wife was either immoral or an incompetent mother. It was assumed that a woman without custody had been disqualified as a parent. And that particular old idea dies hard. The aura of suspected inadequacy still clings to these women. Today, women who are *electing* to live apart from their children are still being treated as though they'd been judged defective.

> *People seemed to feel sorry for me. They assumed that since my children weren't living with me that I must have lost custody. They couldn't imagine that I'd given them up voluntarily.*

> *It's been a known fact that children remain with their mothers. If they didn't, it was for horrendous reasons. There's a big stigma*

attached to it. I can imagine what a mother goes through when a court rules the children should live with the father. And I guess I still tend to think that the court will rule in favor of the mother, unless there are real black marks against her.

When my husband and I split and I learned there was a third party involved, I was hurt and enraged, and I said he could have the house, the kids, and his girlfriend, and I moved out. When I cooled down a little, I knew I wanted the kids to come with me; but they didn't want to leave the house and their school and the neighborhood, and I didn't want to force them. So now the story is that I'm having an affair and that's why I moved out and left my children. In fact, he was the one who hooked up with somebody else, of course. People are so vicious. They can be.

The fear of censure and the suspicion of aberration are greatly exacerbated by the fact that most women experience their feelings about being apart from their children in complete isolation. Even those women who are able to reach the point of deciding to live apart from their children usually do so without knowing anyone else who has chosen this course. And the sense of operating in a vacuum certainly feeds the feeling of unacceptability.

My God, I thought, there must be something wrong with me. I don't know anyone else who's doing this.

I was sure I was the only one who'd ever had these thoughts. That can really make you feel like a monster.

This is still a terrible taboo. There's a Mothers Without Children group in the city where I live, but the woman who's running it has had so much trouble trying to sustain membership that she's almost decided to give it up. Going through traditional channels like newspapers, radio, television to reach women on this issue just doesn't work. They're afraid to come out and be public about it. This is as big a closet issue as homosexuality. No, actually it's bigger than that. Homosexuality is already out of the closet.

The Loss of Identity

Still another reason why women are reluctant to separate from their children is that their connection with their children is the cornerstone of their identity. Motherhood is the crucial component of their self-definition. To part with that component would be to relinquish their very selves. These women may not necessarily want to live with their children. Still, it is unthinkable even to consider letting them go. What would they do without them? What would they put in their place? Their maternity is their identity. Without it, they feel, they would have nothing.

> *I was raised to be a wife and a mother. That's what I was trained for. I never even thought about doing anything else. My parents made it clear that the best thing in the world that could happen to me was to find some man who could take care of me, marry him, and have his children. And that's what I did. So when the time came that I began to think of giving all that up, the husband and the children, it was pretty terrifying. What would I* be *if I wasn't a mother? I'd never even been myself. I'd just been this role: MOTHER.*

> *I had absolutely no sense of who or what I might be apart from my children—really none. I'd just, unquestioningly, been their mother. That was it. That was me. I never had to look beyond that. When the time came that I did, it was pretty scary.*

> *You have to be prepared for anger from the child you allow to go. You have to be prepared for people who just cannot adjust to a new style of living and who will believe you're a bad mother. They will look at you in a way that will make you very uncomfortable. And if you've used your child, if you've hidden behind him, you'll quickly have to find another role. If you brought up the child and made all the decisions, it's very hard to turn that over to someone else. And, if you turn it over, where does that leave you?*

Many of the women we came to know expressed the feeling that parting from their children was like calling their own bluff. They had ambitions that lay beyond the wife/mother role, but they had used that role to keep themselves from pursuing other goals. I can't do it now because of the kids, they would tell themselves. If only I didn't have the kids, think what I could be doing, they would say. These women recognized that parting from their children was also parting with a convenient excuse. They knew they were giving up a safe hiding place.

> *For years I'd been telling myself that the only reason I didn't really become too absorbed with my art work was that the demands the kids made on me were too great, and I couldn't really do both things well, so I'd just do one. But after the kids were gone, I could see what a smokescreen that whole thing had been. I hadn't become absorbed with my art work because I didn't want to put myself on the line. I was afraid to. And that fear was still there long after the kids had gone.*

> *My kids were my cover for years. As long as I was their mother I didn't have to address anything else I might be. But finally that didn't work for me anymore. I knew when they went to live with their father that I'd have to face myself. I guess I was ready to or I wouldn't have let the kids go.*

But what about women who don't suffer from any of the aforementioned liabilities? Women whose identities are not synonymous with their maternity. Women who are able to buck their conditioning. Women who manage, even in a judgmental climate, to make an unpopular choice and change the direction of their lives. Such women do exist, of course. They have approached the decision to live apart from their children in a positive fashion and been certain that the choice they were making was the best for everyone: mother, father, and children. But even *these* women are not immune to the devastation that can be generated by being at odds with the cultural stereotype of what a mother is—and is not.

> *I knew I'd made the right choice. I never even questioned that again once I finally made the decision. But even so I had some pretty uneasy moments. I didn't want people to think badly of me. Who does want that? It's painful.*

If I'd been going by other people's opinions, I would never have left my kids with their father in the first place. I had some support for that but not all that much. So outside judgments weren't that important to me. But that doesn't mean that I just sailed right through it. I was really struck by how little understanding there was of my situation. I knew I'd done the best thing for all of us, but a lot of the time I felt like I was the only one who knew it. My biggest fear is that my children won't understand that I love them. I do everything I can to make my love obvious to them, but that possibility still frightens me. Let's face it, they don't see any other kids living without their mothers. So why are they the only ones? I want them to know that not living with them doesn't mean I'm rejecting them.

Cover Stories

In the past, one way of dealing with what was considered horrendous was to concoct a story to cover it.

I remember the first time I told a lie, and then I lived the lie forever. I said my husband had been killed in an automobile accident and that my children lived with his brother down in Virginia on a farm. I just couldn't have explained to someone in 1958 that my children were living with their father. That was the most difficult part of the whole thing, trying to explain to people, lying. So eventually I stopped saying anything, and the new people I met never even knew I had children.

Attitudes have changed enough in our society to make the big-lie technique passé but not enough to free women to speak openly about the choice they have made. The voices of non-custodial mothers who have made this choice are still muffled.

I didn't tell many people. I have friends who still don't know that I have children.

I wouldn't tell just anyone. I monitor who I tell pretty carefully.

I usually don't volunteer the information that I don't live with my children. And there was a sort of decree issued in my family that the children would never be mentioned to me or my mother, that it would make us too unhappy.

I always feel that I have to explain, and that makes me so angry. Why should I have to do that? I'd rather keep quiet about it.

I haven't talked about this much to a lot of people. Even when people are polite, you sense other things going on underneath.

Two women with whom we spoke had done studies for their doctoral dissertations of mothers living apart from their children. Each reported that she had had difficulty finding women willing to talk to her. Women were reluctant, they both said, for two reasons. One was the fear of being identified. There was a great investment in keeping this aspect of their lives a secret. The other reason was that they didn't want to undergo the pain involved in reexamining their situations. They knew that reliving the past was bound to stir up old agonies. They also feared they might uncover new ones.

Both of *us* certainly understood this. Many times during the work on this book, we came up against hurtful reminders, haunting memories. It is not easy for any of us to walk again over the traumatic territory in our lives. On the other hand, it's a mistake to think that silence really solves anything. Our histories, articulated or not, are there in our present lives, affecting us, adding to the sum total of who we are. Surely it's better to acknowledge them.

Reality, Past and Present

Yet another factor that helps to shape attitudes toward noncustodial mothers often lies buried in our own childhood experiences. No one will argue against the proposition that children need good and consistent care. For most of us, the dispenser of that care was our mother. She was the central, constant presence. Our father was the breadwinner who appeared in our lives mainly in the evenings and on weekends. If *our* mother had been absent, we would have been deprived of care. And that is the equation we carry over into our judgments in the present: if mother isn't there, no one is. The reality, of course, is quite different. The children of the mothers we're talking about *are* receiving care and they are receiving it from a parent.

> *I could see the reaction on people's faces—the nonunderstanding, the horror, judging me as a failure. They don't understand that my children are being taken care of. I didn't desert them, leave them in a dark and desolate place. I didn't abandon them. They're in a loving, caring home, their* father's, *for God's sake.*
>
> *My own fantasy when my son went to live with his father was that he was lying alone in the dark, crying, and no one was there to hear him. That's what it would have meant if my own mother wasn't there when I was little. But the reality is that his father provides him with a very nice life—a house, a dog, dinner, attention, love. My terror about his welfare had more to do with my own history than with present reality.*

The Search for a Norm

When we see, or hear of, a mother without her children, all the connotations seem negative. Mother minus children equals emotional effacement. The situation seems to symbolize an experience without love, without caring, without involvement. Yet what have we really described by saying that a mother lives apart from her children? We have described a living arrangement, nothing more. We have not said how much a mother loves her child, how interested or involved she is in her child's life, what her motives may have been for arriving at the arrangement. We have not defined an emotional relationship—we have simply indicated that a mother and child reside in different places.

But we think we know all sorts of things when we hear of such a mother; we think we know what kind of woman she is, how she came to be apart from her child, what her relationship with her child is like, how her child will be affected by her absence. We conjure up all these things very readily. In fact, all we really know is the rough equivalent of a street address. And that doesn't tell us much.

In the course of researching and writing this book, we came across no evidence that these mothers who chose to live apart from their chilren were "unnatural" women. We found no distinguishing characteristics in their histories that marked them for this path. They came from happy and unhappy childhoods. Some had close relations with their parents, others distant. Early in their children's lives they may have relished the maternal role or disliked it. Their motives in choosing to live apart from their children were loving or selfish, sometimes a mixture of both. They lived in cities and small towns in all regions of this country and came from Jewish, Catholic, and Protestant backgrounds. There were women who'd earned advanced degrees and those with high-school diplomas. Some described themselves as feminists, others did not. Some had experienced therapy, some had not.

We did discover that this issue appears to concern the working, middle, and upper middle classes more than it does the rich or the poor. This is most likely because both of those classes have built-in alternatives to the mother as primary caretaker. The rich have nurses and boarding schools to tend to the children. The poor often live in extended-family households that include grandparents, aunts, and cousins who may care for the children in their mother's place.

But the primary thing the two of us learned in a statistical sense was that these women are virtually indistinguishable from other women of the same age who live *with* their children. These are "normal" women who are struggling to make their way in a complex and changing world. They are women who have made an extremely difficult choice and done so with very little help. They are pioneers who received no applause for their ground-breaking efforts but, rather, continue to pay a high price for them. They are the ones who suffered the pains of being in on something at the beginning.

For surely one day, the idea of a woman living apart from her children will seem neither catastrophic nor deplorable. It will be commonplace. We will truly believe, not just in theory but in practice as well, that a father can be a tender, nurturing parent, sensitive to his children's needs, both physical and emotional, just as surely as a mother can. We will truly believe that mother does *not* necessarily know best.

Most people would agree that an intact family is the best environment in which children can grow up. But an increasing divorce rate has become a reality in our society. And one of the realities of divorce is that one parent changes his or her place of residence and no longer lives with the children full-time. Myths and assumptions aside, is it really any worse if the parent who leaves is the mother?

THREE

The Decision

The ideal criteria for deciding custody would be those that determined which parent, based upon desire, schedule, and personality, is more able, prepared, and eager to do the primary caretaking. In fact, in this less than ideal life, custody decisions are rarely made on the basis of such admirable standards. Life is seldom so tidy, but we did encounter, during the course of our interviews, some instances that came close to meeting the ideal.

Our focus in this book is on women who have chosen to live apart from their children. Some women make this decision at the time of divorce. Others may live with their children in the postdivorce period and decide at a later time to let the children live with their father. The decision is one that women approach from many different avenues.

Occasionally, an overriding factor is evident in the decision-making process. More often, a mixture of factors has determined the choice. Many of these women have approached the matter of their children's custody in a thoughtful, well-reasoned way. A few have exploded out of troublesome marriages in too much pain to think very clearly about anything. Some women are able to be extremely direct about their purpose and the needs and desires underlying it; others need to obscure their motives, even from themselves. These motives are often loving, sometimes selfish, rarely simple. Each of these women's stories is wholly idiosyncratic, yet certain common threads tie many of them together.

Financial Strains

One of these recurrent threads is economic, and its importance cannot be overstated. The income of single-mother homes is estimated to be less than half that of single-father homes. Women's salaries, on the average, are just slightly more that half those of men. In a study of single mothers that asked the question, "What is your greatest worry as a single mother?" the most common response was "Money." Single mothers who work often find the dual roles of major breadwinner and primary caretaker exhausting. And the awful double bind for these women is that even as they struggle long and hard to meet their children's physical needs, they feel, due to their finite resources of time and energy, that their children's psychological and emotional needs are being overlooked. Women who cited financial reasons as the primary cause of relinquishing their children were most often mothers who had retained custody of their children at the time of the divorce but found, after a period of single motherhood, that the strain was too great.

> *At the time of my divorce I had five children, from four to eleven, and they were with me. I was working as an alcoholism counselor. A few years after the divorce we had to move, and I ended up with astronomical rent. Then here's the position I was in: if I worked, my kids would have a roof over their heads, but I wouldn't be home; but if I was home and there for them continually, they wouldn't have a roof or food. Not very good choices. So I muddled along, but my job was suffering, my health was suffering, and the kids were coming off the walls. Close friends were helpful to me because they said "Look, how long are you going to beat your head against the wall? Maybe it's time to be strong by being weak and saying enough is enough." So I went to my ex-husband, who was in a position to help, and told him he'd either have to give me more financial support or take the kids, and he said he'd take the kids. Money was a big factor. If I'd been in a better financial position, I would have kept them.*

Financially, I went under. I had my three kids living with me for six years after the divorce, and it was just too hard finally. I felt very guilty that we were living on rice and vegetables and granola. Now everyone's vegetarian, but they weren't then, and we were doing it from economic necessity. And all of us had jobs; everyone had to contribute so that we were able to live in a big house and have bikes and sneakers. Even the nine-year-old had two jobs. But none of that was true when they went to live with their daddy and stepmother. I was glad for them. At one point their father was head of a school in the Middle East, and they lived there for eleven months. They toured Europe for another five months. Living with him has had benefits beyond my greatest dreams for them. When I think of that, I know I did the right thing.

One woman who tried mixing work with single motherhood feels very strongly that these are simply mutually incompatible endeavors.

If women want to go back into the work force, they need the time to do it. Kids need a parent to be around. You can't have a career and children at the same time if you're just starting your career and do justice to either one. You have to decide what's most important. If women want to work they have to be prepared to leave their children, and that's very hard, very painful. The women's movement does women a disservice by telling them they can have both simultaneously. It's really addressing itself to the upper end of the economic scale, not to women who are working like beasts really, working all day for low wages and then coming home at night and taking care of kids and a house.

Some single mothers who didn't work also experienced a sense of financial pressure.

I had the children with me for a year and a half, and it was very difficult to live as a single parent. Child support and alimony didn't stretch far enough. It was hard to maintain the house physically. I was barely making it. When my ex would come to take the children, I'd ask him to get them haircuts, or I'd point out a hole in a sneaker. But instead of helping me out with these essentials, he'd take them to a toy store and spend forty dollars on something frivolous. Then, of course, the kids would say how much they liked being with Daddy. So when I finally got exasperated with hearing them say that and tired of saying no to them when they wanted things, no to myself when I wanted something, I decided I'd try them living with him. We did it on a six-month trial basis and it worked.

These are instances in which a mother felt she was simply not able to provide adequately for her children, and she determined that their father might be better able to carry the financial burden. But interestingly, even when women cited other issues as more important in the decision-making process, financial strain was often present as well.

Stability During Trauma

Another common theme in many stories was the mother's desire to provide the maximum amount of stability for her children at a most unstable time of their lives, the time of divorce itself.

I had known for many years that my marriage wasn't good, but we still had managed to provide a loving home for our kids. I'd always known I would leave as soon as my youngest was in college, but instead I left when he was fifteen because it was getting to the point where I couldn't bear it anymore. When I told my husband that I was going to leave, I also told him he could have custody of the child because I thought that was best. I considered my husband a good parent. He couldn't fulfill my emotional needs, but he's a good father, a good role model. And of all our children, he loved the youngest most. My son doesn't like change of any kind, and I thought the best thing for him was to have his mother out of the house but everything else exactly the same. If he'd come with me he would've had to change schools, and I had a new job that involved lots of travel, and he would have been alone a lot. This way the only change was that I no longer lived in the same house. I stayed nearby though and spent a few days a week with him.

At the time of our divorce I had a job in executive recruiting in the city and my husband was a schoolteacher in the suburbs. We had two eight-year-old daughters. Also, I was planning to remarry. I felt if he had custody, which he wanted, it wouldn't be so traumatic for the children. They could stay in their own house, keep their own friends. He'd be home in the afternoon after school. Those were all things that they couldn't have if they came with me.

At the end of my marriage I was working in the city full time in a very good job, and I left the house at seven in the morning and got home at seven-thirty at night, so I was seeing very little of the children as it was. Working was a great fulfillment for me. We had tried to avert the divorce. We'd been in family therapy. But it just wasn't working out. At one point my older boy said to me he didn't know why his father and I stayed together, we were so unhappy, and why didn't we get a divorce? Finally, my husband's attitude was that he wouldn't leave the house or the children, and if I wanted to leave I could go.

I knew we could go through a tremendous legal fight, and I could probably have ended up having the kids with me during the week, but what would I have gained? Taking them to the city with me would have been horrendous culture shock for them, I felt, and where would we live and where would they go to school and all those other questions like that. Also, I considered my husband, and still do, a very good father who cares very much for his children. They're his whole life, in fact; he has very few friends.

So gradually over the course of nearly a year, I came to think we all might be better off if I had the kids on weekends. That was the time when I'd be relaxed and have time to spend and could really enjoy them. So we settled on joint custody, the kids spending weekends and summers in the city with me. Also, I agreed to contribute to child support. We presented our decision to the children as a fait accompli, a very positive thing: it would be best for them to stay with their father because I was moving to the city and then they'd come to me on weekends. They seemed fine with it. I think they were relieved and glad to have it settled.

I didn't feel I was leaving my children, nor do I feel now that I've given them up or lost them. I just felt that I'd be seeing them in a different time frame with a much better quality of time.

I had converted to Catholicism and met the man who was to be my second husband. He'd been a monk and we were planning to form a spiritual community. I just didn't feel that there was any question of taking the children with me. They were sixteen, fifteen, and thirteen, girls with a boy in the middle. They were happy in school and with the neighborhood situation. My husband was a good father, and he was planning to remarry. I didn't want to uproot them, and I didn't see how I could take them. I think the situation was solved in the best way for the children.

Women at Work

The matter of work was at the heart of many women's decisions. Some were just on the brink of careers and felt they needed the time and space to get established without the twin burdens of financial pressure and full-time parental responsibility. Others were continuing time-and-energy-demanding careers that existed during their marriages. Some were in school, preparing themselves for careers to come.

When I first got married I dropped out and played housewife and mother for two-and-a-half years until I went crazy. Then I began to work my way out and back into the work world. I was living in New England, and a job came up in the capital city of my state. I knew if I took that job my life would never be the same, and it hasn't been. I'm a working person, and my career helps to define me. For the first six months I commuted between the capital and home. Then my husband and two daughters joined me. But my life was hectic. I traveled all the time, and I spent very little time with the family. My daughters adjusted amazingly though, and that had a lot to do with my decision to leave them with my husband when we separated. He's a solid, nurturing person, a wonderful father and a wonderful man. He has another woman in his life now, and he belongs in the house. He's happy there. I've made a complete break now in terms of spending day-to-day time with my kids who are now twelve and thirteen. But my gift to them is that I won't resent what I gave up for them.

I'd like to think that the time I'm not spending with them now I'll spend with them later.

I married when I was nineteen years old and had sole custody of my kids for eight years. All my overachieving friends had been working and establishing careers, and I'd always thought of myself as "just a mother." All of them were telling me I was so lucky to have had my kids and have that behind me because their biological clocks were running down and now it was time for them to have children. Anyway, I wanted a career, and I had a good opportunity presented to me to begin one; and I felt it was my ex-husband's turn to have the kids who were thirteen and nine. He agreed. He said I deserved some time. He said, "You've been a mother since you were twenty, and you're thirty-four now, and it's time for you to take your life into your own hands. Let me have the children, and I'll give them a secure, loving environment, and you'll see them all the time." I thought that was a marvelous idea, even though it terrified me. After all, being a mother was all I knew.

When my husband and I separated, we were living in the Southwest, near the mountains. I took our daughter and moved to the nearest city. I was living on food stamps and welfare, and I started becoming involved with the community theater there, and that was the beginning of my life. I wasn't being paid, but I loved the work. I knew this was what I wanted to do. Eventually, my husband moved into an apartment next door to mine and that seemed hopeful. I thought we could work something out about sharing the care of our daughter, but it was a fiasco. He didn't help at all. He finally moved out and, with another woman, went back to where we had been living.

One day my daughter woke up and said, "Mommy, I'm hungry"; and I had no food and no money, and I took her to him and told him to take care of her, and I left. I was destroyed and sobbing, in really bad shape. I didn't hear from him for a couple weeks, and then we tried to talk. I'd never had the chance to do anything in my life, I told him. I needed some time. I asked him to keep her for a while; he said he wanted to, but the woman he was living with, whom he planned to marry, was somewhat bitter about being saddled with a child and said they would only take her if I gave them full custody. I balked but I also realized that I wanted a career. I didn't want to be just a mother. And I couldn't manage a career and a child by myself with no support from him. So I agreed. I was happy that my daughter would have a home. He'd always loved her very much, and he's bloomed into a wonderful father. I felt good about my daughter being in a family situation.

I had gone back to school during my marriage, and at the time we separated I was contemplating getting my Ph.D. in clinical psychology. My children were ten and eight and five, and if they were with me I felt they'd be with babysitters a lot of the time. Also, going through that Ph.D. program is very rigorous, and I felt I'd resent them if they took my time away from it. I felt my husband was a good parent. His relations with the children are better than with adults. The kids are the most important part of his life. They always were. He's affectionate. I didn't see how I could ask for a divorce and for the house and the kids. I didn't see how I could do that to him. I couldn't get everything. I felt if he had the kids I'd be able to see them and maintain a good relationship with them.

The decision to live apart from my children really came about quite organically. I'd been divorced five years, and the kids had been living with me. At first, we'd stayed in our house in the suburbs, then we moved into the city. My ex-husband had always wanted to raise them, and he'd brought the idea up many times, but I wouldn't hear of it. He was pretty much like a clucking mother in some ways. He was a nurturing type, and he did want to be involved with the kids. I wasn't like that at all. I always wanted to be out of the house. It was hard for me to be home. I'd always had housekeepers. I would rather have a good housekeeper than a husband. I'm very career-oriented with a very definite purpose and a strong drive to express who I am and why I'm here.

Anyway, every once in a while my ex-husband would mention the possibility of his taking the kids, but I wasn't ready for that yet, for that sort of freedom, and I'd say no. I was still hiding behind the role of motherhood. Then one day I began to think of it, and I realized I felt ready. The next day he called and asked me again, and we practically settled the whole thing on the phone. We discussed it with the kids, who were eleven and nine then, and it felt okay to them to go with their father. They wanted to move out of the city. They missed their old friends, their old school. And it was time for me to move out and spread my wings. I really needed the freedom then.

My ex-husband is a good father who feels love for his children and expresses it. He takes the role of parent very seriously. He sees their teachers at school. He watches them do their homework. He's a good disciplinarian, much better than I was. We have very different value systems, and I wish he were more developed spiritually, but he's a good father. There's no question of that.

It took a great deal of courage for me to let go of the role of mother, which had given me my identity. I'd never been alone in my life. What a lot of women do, what I did, is to hide behind the traditional role of mother, and therefore we never have to try to exercise our full creativity and power. If we don't try to do anything else we can always fall back on our role and say, "I am a mother." The time finally came for me to step beyond that.

Establishing Identity

It is clear that work is extremely important to these women, just as much a part of their self-definition as their motherhood. But sometimes a woman's need to define herself cannot be encompassed by a particular career or work goal. It may be far more subtle and far less specific than that. But, the need can be powerful, and valid. This seems to be particularly true of women who have married young and submerged their identities in the lives of their husbands and children. These women may at first need time apart from everyone else to establish a sense of their own identity. Only then can they consider what their life's work might be.

We'd been married sixteen years when problems started arising between us, and at the same time I was aware of the growing difficulty I was having with motherhood. I had always felt it too overwhelmingly. I was too involved in my kids' lives; their ups and downs were my ups and downs. At the same time, I didn't enjoy being at home once the kids were beyond the ages of three and five. As soon as I could get babysitters for them, I was off taking classes and that sort of thing. It seems I spent a lot of time away from home.

But even so, when I began to recognize that my husband and I were going to split up, it never occurred to me that I might have the option not to take the children. That's just something a woman doesn't do. Then at one point my husband said to me, "If you want to finish me off then take the children too." And that's when it started occurring to me that I didn't want to take the children. It occurred to me that I didn't want to fight for them, and I didn't want the responsibility.

Just at this time my husband was transferred abroad, where we'd always wanted to go, and we decided we wouldn't split yet but go abroad as a family. We thought maybe it would be good for us. But it wasn't long before we realized that that was a drastic mistake and that there was no way we could hold the family together. The kids were nine and eleven then. So I said I'd move to the city and leave the kids with him. He had a beautiful house in the countryside, resources to hire someone to come in and do the shopping and tending and so forth, and the kids were settled in schools near there. Also, my husband had been very much involved in the children's growth in their earliest years, and that had continued on. It wasn't as if I was leaving them with a man who was indifferent.

So on the surface there were many practical reasons for this choice, and it may seem to have been a practical decision. But it really had much more to do with what I was feeling inside. What had happened was that subtly and slowly over a period of time I began to realize that this was an option and that it actually appealed to me. I began to envision how my life could be, and I kept that vision in my mind. Yes, all the practical considerations were real, but when it came to the bottom line, I checked what was going on inside of me and everything inside me said this really appeals to me, this is right for me. There is another way of living, and I'm going to live it.

I'd never had a chance to define my life in my terms. I'd gone from father to husband without missing a beat. I hate that label of a woman doing her own thing. I absolutely abhor it, but someone hearing me might say that's what I was doing. I don't see it quite that way. I saw it as a decision that was best for all of us.

I could recognize that I needed to be on my own for a while. I moved into a place I knew was too small for the children. I knew they wouldn't be comfortable there, and yet I chose it. That showed me how I was thinking. When I was with my children, I gave a lot to them and that was an escape for me. I got very busy with the mother role—cooking, cleaning, washing, running around—and there was no time to look at who I was, where I was. I put all my energies into looking after them, and I was strictly a caretaker. I had nothing left over to be their playmate, their companion. I tend to get lost in other people's needs. It's sort of an out for me. I become very involved in attending to everyone else's needs and that way I don't have to look at myself. But on my own I'm forced to look at who I am and what I'm about and what's going on with me. And that's something I've never done. I have a lot to work out.

More unusual, but not unheard of, is the woman who is very clear about her priorities long before the time of separation and divorce.

I had a career before I was married and during my marriage, and I made an agreement with my husband even before our child was born that if we split the child was going with him. I hadn't known anyone who'd made that choice, but I hadn't needed to have the example either. It was my decision, and I'm happy with it. The career has come first with me. It's always come first. And the child is better off with my ex-husband.

Fathers Are Parents, Too

In some instances, one of the most important considerations in a mother's decision was the stated desire of the children's father to have his kids live with him. There are cases, certainly, where this may merely be a cover for a husband's wish to punish his soon-to-be-ex-wife. He may be more eager to deprive his wife of the children than he actually is to have the children himself. But, we found many instances in which the father's desire for his children was genuine, something the mothers recognized and took into account.

The father is a blood parent too, after all, though that fact seems to have been ignored often in the past. Some women who cited this as a major consideration said unequivocally that they felt their children's father would be a better parent than they would. Others felt very strongly that a father should not be robbed of the experience of knowing his children on a day-to-day basis. These women may turn over custody to their children's father after having had it awhile themselves, or they may relinquish it at the time of divorce, feeling they have already put in substantial time raising and becoming acquainted with their children.

I decided some time ago that my kids would be better off with their father, and he wants full custody. He's very steady. He's the rock. He interacts with them better than I do. I work well with them one-to-one but not as a group. I also felt I'd be better off alone because I'm in school and going on to graduate school. I love my kids, but I feel they'd be better off with him.

I had my three kids for the first two years after our separation. They were two, five, and six, all boys. Then I remarried. Shortly after that my new husband was arrested for something I knew nothing about. It was a real bad situation, and I sent my two oldest kids to spend the summer with my ex-husband while I kept the baby. I was trying to get the marriage annulled and was flying back and forth between the East and West Coasts, and finally my ex and I sat down and he said, "Let me take the kids and you get yourself together, and as soon as you're ready, they'll come back to you. We won't make any legal changes. We'll just agree on it." We both agreed it was best for the kids. When I did it I didn't know it would be permanent, but even when we were all finally living in the same city again they continued living with him because I didn't have a place to live. I didn't have a job. But I saw them any time I wanted to and spent every weekend with them.

My spouse asked if he could have the children, and I said yes. It just came out of the blue, but this seemed like a lifeline that was being thrown to me. My kids were two and a half and three and a half, and I was physically, mentally, and emotionally drained. I remember saying to my mother before this was even in my mind, I said, "Mom, some days I wish I could just get on a bus and keep going and never come back." And she said, "If you do that you'll cry yourself to sleep at night." Well, I didn't get on a bus, but I did go and I haven't cried myself to sleep every night though there have certainly been times.

I think it was the right decision, and there were a lot of factors. Finances were one thing; he had a good job. He was a good father. He had lots of relatives who would be willing to babysit and help him out. I only had my mother, and the kids were driving her crazy. And I was wiped out; I couldn't take anymore. But even with all that I don't think I would have approached him and asked for him to take the children. It was his idea and that may have made it a little easier for me.

It was my husband's idea that the children live with him. He wanted them very much, and he's involved with a woman who's really into the kids. He probably would have gone to court to get them, and I knew that and I knew he had a pretty strong case against me. I'd had some drug problems, though that was behind me by that time, and during one of our separations I'd had an affair with someone. I talked to my therapist and to a few close friends, and I decided not to go through that. I decided the only way I could win at all in this situation was to let him have the kids because he really did want them and to give the kids quality time when I did see them. I feel I took the easiest route for happiness for the kids and for me.

I left my husband when our son was two. I was just twenty-one years old, and I went on welfare and went to school full time. Just as I was finishing school, my son was about to start school, and his father came to me and asked if his son could live with him. I'd never thought of the idea before. I'd just assumed he'd live with me, but I thought it was a good idea. Intellectually, I thought it was fair: he's half his kid, after all. Also, I'd just finished school and wasn't sure what I'd be doing. My ex-husband, who was an established musician, was in a more stable situation than I was. And he's a good father. Otherwise I wouldn't let the child be with him. After we split up, my ex-husband was always diligent about his son, really into him, trying to see him as much as he could, taking him places. He always took care of him and he had a lot of free time. Also, once he presented the idea I realized I might like the freedon, I might like being not so tied down.

When my son was born I was enthralled. He was beautiful, gorgeous. But I felt very inadequate to the task of caring for him. I was afraid I would hurt him. My husband made me feel I could never do anything right with him. He had a very strong bond with our son right from the beginning. He loved him a lot and that was lovely. So there were things about it that were marvelous to me, but I also felt overwhelmed. I felt very enclosed. All that there was there for me in my life was staying at home and being with my child. I was just nineteen years old and that wasn't enough. I felt very cut off from the world. I felt I needed more stimulation.

I kept thinking that there had to be more, that this couldn't be what life was going to be like. And finally, after two and a half years, I left. My reading at the time was that my husband was much more competent to look after our son than I was. He seemed to me more stable than I was, more able to be there for our son than I was. And he wanted him. He made that very clear. Also I didn't have the financial resources to set up a viable household. I couldn't have supported my son adequately. But the main thing was that I couldn't have provided him with the stability that he found in his father's home. It was the only decision I could have made.

Part of Her Own Past

One woman we interviewed, whose husband was eager to have his daughter live with him, had had the experience of living with her own father while she was growing up. This had been a very positive experience for her, and that fact certainly influenced her decision regarding her own daughter.

I was going to leave the East and move to the West Coast. I knew I just had to be out of urban surroundings and into a whole new environment. The city was too rough for me. But I'd had custody of my daughter for a year and a half since our divorce, and I had every intention of taking her with me. She was three at the time. Her father was very upset when I told him this. He said it seemed unfair that I'd fostered this closeness between him and his child, which I had, and now I was going to take her three thousand miles away. He said, "You can't do this to me. You can't leave and take my money [for child support] and take my child and have me never see her. It's just not fair." And I couldn't say that it was fair because it wasn't.

There were several really difficult months while we tried to decide what to do. My ex-husband and I had some terrible fights. He was pretty determined I wasn't going to go and take her, so it really became a decision of whether or not I should go at all because it became clear that I couldn't go and take her without a fight.

My parents had been divorced when I was fifteen, and I stayed with my father so I had a sense that being brought up by your father wasn't such a bad deal. We had a wonderful time, my father and I. We became quite close. We really had to rely on each other to pull off this kind of unacceptable situation. The neighbors didn't approve, friends didn't approve, the school didn't approve. Children were supposed to be with their mother, especially girls. So our attitude was, okay, we'll show them. And we got together and showed them. My father became really a dear friend as well as a parent. We talked about things. We talked about everything. So when the time came for me to deal with this with my daughter, that helped me to decide.

I talked to a number of women friends in my neighborhood who were very supportive. These were women immersed in traditional families with several children and they said, "Go for it . . . your daughter will be fine, you'll have a chance to do your art work, to settle yourself in a new place." Their voices were the loudest to me because I thought they'd be the people who would disapprove the most.

Another factor was that my daughter and her father had a very strong, nurturing relationship. He's really a good mother and I'm not. I'm a great father. I loved the first year of motherhood, but then it began to wear thin for me. I liked babies but had a hard time with toddlers. I loved my daughter, but I didn't really enjoy her company.

It was a terrible, wrenching thing but we decided to try it for six months and then she'd come to be with me the following summer. When she came in June I was in good shape, she was in good shape, and my ex-husband was in good shape. It began to seem that it was going to work all right. And it has. The three thousand miles are the worst part, but otherwise I wouldn't have changed anything. I think we did it as well as it could have been done.

Separation Anxiety

Another woman sensed that she might be able to deal more effectively with separation from her children than their father could, and that became a primary consideration in her decision-making.

Initially, I had no positive feelings about leaving the kids. The idea of being without them was frightening to me, terrifying really. I couldn't imagine not being with my kids. That just wasn't part of my vision. When I realized that divorce was the only option for us, I just assumed that I would be the custodial parent. But I also wanted a divorce that wouldn't shred the family apart. By family I mean not just our nuclear family of four but my in-laws, my parents, a whole network of relationships, very meaningful ones, that I didn't want to die because of the divorce. The whole idea of family and pride in family was important to both my husband and me.

He said to me at one point in a joint counseling session, "You're not going to completely destroy my family. The boys stay with me in the house." And he made it very clear that he would fight for that. I perceived that this threatened custody battle was not just a way to get at me. It wasn't a statement that he didn't have confidence in me as a parent. I began to see that he was absolutely terrified of being left alone and that he wanted to maintain whatever family structure he could. Given this and my very strong feeling about wanting to keep relationships as intact as possible with families on both sides, I could see that a big fat bloody custody battle was just not part of my plan. Basically he's a very good father. There are a few aspects of his parenting which trouble me a little bit, but he's very steady, very stable. He has a great deal of integrity, and I trust him completely. I felt that he couldn't handle losing the kids. I felt I had resources to deal with that that he didn't have.

Doing What the Kids Want

Occasionally, and usually when older children are involved, the children's desires may influence a woman's custody decision. Often the children are reluctant to leave their familiar environment, their school, their friends. Many women noted that this was a factor they took into account.

I had lived in the suburbs all during my marriage, which lasted nineteen years, and I found the suburbs a real drag. These were educated people, but they had such small minds. It seemed nobody read a newspaper; no one communicated about things going on in the outside world. Before my marriage I'd been a senior progammer in a large urban firm, and I wanted to return to the city and to that career when I separated from my husband. My five children were ages eighteen through four, the two oldest, girls, the others boys.

We told the children one by one, except for the youngest, and I wanted to take the children, but the two girls said they didn't want to come with me. They had friends where they were, their school. They'd grown up there; they didn't want to go to the city. And I decided not to split up the family. I thought it might be less traumatic if they stayed together. And the children didn't ask me to stay nearby in the suburbs. They knew I was unhappy. They knew I was uptight. They could see the whole thing coming.

When I began to think of divorce I was planning to take the children, and I was sort of hurt when the two girls said no, but then I came to understand. And now that they know more about the city than they did then, they say in some ways maybe they made the wrong decision. If the children had been much younger I probably wouldn't have asked what they felt; I would just have taken them. Also, if I'd been younger I probably would have demanded the children. I didn't feel that strongly about myself then; I didn't feel I was that important. But, as it was, the decision to be without them was really the children's. If they'd wanted to come, I would have taken them.

I was divorced shortly after my son was born, and I raised him alone until he was fourteen. Now for the last year he's been living with his father. My son suggested going to his father, something I'd never even thought of because his father had played very little part in his life. We lived in the East, and he lived outside a midwestern city and was remarried and had two other children. But it seemed like it might be a good idea. It had become very difficult for my son and me to live together. We were constantly embattled to the point where I think it was affecting my health. He gets along well with his father, and I felt his father could give him a different balance than he had here, a different structure. I felt that being in a family with two other children and two adults, he'd have to cooperate. His father was willing. I think he thought this was his last chance to develop any relationship with his son.

On the one hand you can't just throw your kid away and say go live with someone else if things get rough. You have to try to work them out. But I really began to feel that his success in his adult life was somewhat dependent on his changing his behavior, and I couldn't help him along those lines. We were entangled in this old relationship, and all he was getting from it was an inabilty to cope with things in appropriate ways. I wanted him to have the chance to grow into a healthy adult, not thinking he was the only person on earth.

I also knew the conflict between us was dragging me down. I guess I felt entitled to make my life a little better too. And children need both parents. I didn't want my son to think I deprived him of the possibility of knowing his father. We decided to try it for a year, and if it didn't work out I'd have him come back. I wouldn't allow him to stay in an environment I felt was bad for him. I just felt from my heart that this would give him a better chance in life.

Both of my daughters lived with me initially when my husband and I began to separate. But when my youngest was sixteen she decided she wanted to live with her father. She's very rebellious and plays on me very effectively. I'm not strong enough for her—that's always been a problem. Her father's much better with her in that respect. When she's with me nothing ever seems to change. We react to each other in a certain way, and that's how it is.

I had custody of my three sons after the divorce, and then I remarried and had another son. At one point I became ill, and my first three sons went to stay with their father for a month. At the end of that time the two oldest ones wanted to come home, but the youngest wanted to stay with his father. He may have thought that with his father he'd be the only one . . . he'd be the baby again. He'd always liked being the baby and was very jealous when my last son was born. So I lost him. It wasn't something the court did. It was something he wanted, and I didn't force the issue.

We had had a somewhat unusual marriage, at least for that time, which was the late sixties, early seventies. Basically I was the steady breadwinner, and my husband stayed home and took care of the house. He also began to build a close relationship with our son, and the real source of his identity became being a father. That's who he was; that's what he was good at. Occasionally he would work at something else, maybe do some substitute teaching, but his real career was in the home. Meanwhile, I was working full time and finishing my dissertation, so I didn't have as much time to spend at home as I would have liked. I began to feel that in some ways my husband pushed me away from being with my son.

When we decided to separate we agreed in principle to joint custody, and we wanted to have a friendly separation. One of us was going to be in the East and the other out West, so that meant that one of us would have our son for three months, the summer, and the other for nine months. The question was who would get him for the nine months? My husband argued that it should be him; I argued it should be me. And what we finally came up with was an agreement that we would alternate years. He was going to have the first year.

I was ill for much of that year with a bad case of mono. I couldn't even hold a paperback book, much less work regularly. And that spring my ex-husband called to say that he wasn't going to honor our agreement, and my son wouldn't be coming back to live with me the following year. Well, as it turned out, he did come because we'd had that in writing. But I didn't have as much time to devote to him as I would have liked. I was still recovering from mono. I was working toward tenure so I had to publish things. I was working very hard to make up for time lost the preceding year.

Meanwhile, his father had given him the picture of a loving, doting father who spent a great deal of time with him and took him swimming and cross-country skiing and things like that. And during the year he spent with me, on his spring break out West, he decided he wanted to live with his dad, and he told me that that's what he wanted to do. So I thought about that for a while and thought I could probably go to court and probably win, but if I did win what would I have? I'd have my child living with me but wanting to be with his father. That wouldn't be a good situation. So I let him go.

When my son was small I felt I could take care of him best. But as he grew it became harder for me to discipline him. I felt he needed his father, and my son wanted to be with him. I trust my ex-husband and his wife. We all want what's best for the child. The last year my son and I were together I was flaring up at him, and he was getting fresh. He seemed to be crying out for a masculine voice of authority.

I was unhappy, with my teaching job, with where I lived, with my social life, everything. I decided to go back to school full-time, and that's been really hard. I felt a real loss of status. I went from having a job, a house, a car, a child, and control of my own life to being just a student with some of my professors younger than I am. It's been a time of floundering around, and I'm glad my child's not here for this. I didn't want to lean on him for support. I think he sensed that, and it's another reason he wanted to be with his father. It's a much more stable, predictable environment at the moment. When he went to live with his father I felt my abiltiy to cope was dwindling, my battery was running down. I felt enough already, I've done my part. Being a single mother is a real survival trip. There's constant pressure and loneliness.

Where my son was living has really been his decision since the time he was about eight years old or so, and I think he would like to have done it even sooner. He's always wanted to run his own life, and he's been lucky enough not to have a horror scene with either parent if he did that. We both wanted him, and we both welcomed him. He was basically with me until he was ten years old. We lived in the city, and during some of that period my ex and I lived in the same building, so he could see either one of us just by getting on the elevator. Then my son and I moved to the country, and he hated it there. He's a very open, alive, independent, responsible kid who never fit in very well in the small town. He'd been in private school in the city and then went to public school in the country, and he didn't like that. So he initiated the idea of going back to live with his father in the city, and I thought he should be where he wanted to be.

I never had any doubt that he would be okay with my ex or with me, and maybe that gave us a certain freedom that some parents don't have. His father was always very committed to being a parent. Our son was born in the labor room while the doctor was off having coffee, and my husband was there and delivered him really. Seeing his child born and being part of it was probably part of that strong bond. The relationship between my son and his father is easier than his and mine in terms of temperament.

Over the Long Haul—or the Short

The theme of single-mother burnout—what might be called the I-can-no-longer-cope syndrome—turned up several times in our interviews. This generally occurred when a divorced mother lived alone with her children, had full responsibility for them, and over the short or long haul found it impossibly difficult. Financial pressure, as noted earlier, often played a part in this feeling of being overwhelmed. The sense of never having enough time certainly added to it. These women felt they were just barely getting by. They had no energy to take enjoyment in the task of being a parent. They were simply concentrating on staying afloat. In many women's stories there's some of this sense of being, at best, overextended or, at worst, stretched to the breaking point, but in some instances it seems to be the entire tale.

I was living in a small town in the South, a nurse married to an anesthesiologist, in a marriage that was all wrong from day one. By the time my son was a year and a half old I was in therapy, and I knew I had to get out of the marriage. I took my son and moved to the big city and got a job. And this is the way my days went: I'd get up a five o'clock in the morning, feed my son, take him to day care, go to work, pick up my son, take him to another day care for the rest of the afternoon, go back to work, get off work, pick up my son, come home, get him dinner, bathe him, put him to bed, and by that time I'd collapse, exhausted. Then I'd get up the next day and start all over again.

I got ill and my son was having physical problems. So I went back to my husband, but that was no good and I left again. But this time I left my son with him. I decided my husband could give him more, financially and emotionally, in every way. I wanted to kill myself, but I wasn't gong to do that so it came down to taking a chance on hurting myself or a two-year-old child who probably didn't even know what was going on. And I decided to take the chance on me because I'm worth it. But it was the hardest decision.

Having my two sons go to live with their father was the second most important point in my life—the first was the divorce—and it was out of sheer desperation. I let them go because I couldn't cope. If I was out two nights a week they'd say, "You're never home." I was tired of saying no. I had no money. It was totally draining in every way to keep them. I needed a breather—I was just so sick of taking care of everyone else and having nothing for myself. Even so, when my husband first offered to take the children I said drop dead. *You know, I'm the mother, I'm supposed to keep the children. Then I started debating with myself about doing it, but I was afraid of my parents' judgment. I had one friend who was a widow and one who was a widower, and they urged me to accept my husband's offer. "Take it," they said. "It's the best offer you'll ever get." They both felt cheated because they felt they didn't have any choice in how their lives turned out. Then my father told me to call my husband's bluff. "He won't be able to handle it," he said. "You'll have them back in two months." So I let them go.*

Leaving It All Behind

We also encountered a few women whose attitude might be described as I-can't-even-*begin*-to-cope. These were women who married young, had children immediately, and knew long before they were divorced that motherhood was not a particularly satisfying experience for them, at least not at that time in their lives. When they separated from their husbands they never even considered taking on custody of their children. They wanted to leave behind them, at the time of separation, everything associated with the role of wife/mother, and that certainly included their children. They are the first to say that what they wanted was flight, pure and simple.

> *I didn't want to be a wife or a mother. I just wanted to run away and play, and that's what I did. I never took responsibility for my child or for myself. At the time I left my son was four years old, and my husband said that if I went I could never have him back. So I knew what the stakes were. But I was so immature at the time, so confused. It's taken me a lot of time in therapy to work this through, but I feel now I'm a totally different person. I've come to terms with who I am as a mother and as a woman. I've also come to understand my underlying motive for running away. I feel I never had a mother. She was a very sick lady, and one of the things I remember from my childhood was her saying to me, "I'm going away and I'm never coming back." I think I used my husband and child to get back at her for that. Now I'm able to go to my son and say I was wrong and tell him it will never happen again, that I'll always be there for him.*

> *My husband was much older than I and totally devoted to our children, but the marriage was very dissatisfying to me. I was eager to get out in the world, get on with life, and as soon as I left he went to court and got custody. I was totally self-centered at that point, completely involved with having a youth that I felt I'd never had. I was really out of it. It took about three or four years for what I'd done to really hit me. at the same time I realized he could probably take much better care of the children than I could. He had money, he was settled, he adored them. And I was just being a hippie and being stupid. At the time it didn't occur to me to get a lawyer and fight for the kids. That seemed like something I could do in the future when things calmed down. Looking back at it now, I think how could I possibly leave a little child—but I did it. I was another person then, a very weak person. I just ran. That was my MO at the time. I can't believe that was me. I'm still not resolved about it all. It's hard to sort out.*

It is interesting to note a few things about these women who come closest to fitting the stereotype of the abandoning, rejecting mother. First, they seem to be a very small minority. Second, they left their children in situations where they knew they would be well cared for. And third, while they could certainly be found guilty of immaturity, of a kind of self-absorption that made them somewhat insensitive to the needs of other people, these were not notably callous, cold, or unfeeling women. Indeed, when some time had passed and growth had occurred, most of them wanted to reestablish relationships with their children and set about doing so.

Plans to Move

Geography is another factor that can play a big part in custody decisions and play it in many different ways. A woman's job may dictate a relocation. The need to find work may cause a woman to move. Sometimes an area that seemed congenial to a woman when she was married is the last place on earth she wants to live as a single person.

> *When my husband and I separated our plan was to maintain joint custody, alternating years in the house. We had two teenagers. The first year I lived with the children. Then the second year he came back into the house and I moved out. We wanted the children to stay in the house and not be uprooted. We figured if anyone was uprooted it should be us. Then I had an opportunity for a job in another part of the country, and it became obvious that he should stay in the house, and the children would stay with him.*

> *My husband and I were living in a small town in upstate New York, and when we separated our son was a year and a half old. He lived one week with me, then one week with his father. Eventually, I realized I wanted to leave this area. There was nothing there for me. No work. I hated the whole social thing as a single person. I just couldn't live there any more. My husband had remarried, and he and his new wife had a perfect sort of life, and I resented that and I just continued to feel worse and worse about myself.*
>
> *I told my ex-husband I wanted to leave and take our son with me.*

He said, "No way. His school's here. His friends are here." We were heading for a custody battle. Then I finally realized I wanted the chance to go off by myself. I wasn't emotionally ready to have the entire responsibility for a child by myself. I really didn't want it. I couldn't even get myself together. Also I knew his father really loved him, that he was stable and could support him. He was a good father.

When I was divorced in the Midwest I had custody of my six-year-old son. Not too long after that I was relocating to an eastern city, and I asked his grandmother if she'd keep him for the school year while I was moving and getting settled. She said she would, but she wanted custody. At first I agreed, then I changed my mind. My husband went to court, charging abandonment, and won custody and has had it ever since.

My relationship with my son from his birth to age six was wonderful, everything I'd ever want. But then I got very preoccupied with the breakup of the marriage, and I lost track of how it was affecting him. I should have been more careful, but I made the wrong move. I was so emotionally uptight at the time. With hindsight I can see the decision was in his best interests, but it seems like I could have figured out something better.

I came to New York from the West to learn a new kind of work for me, television production. I was doing this with my husband's consent. He paid for the trip. It was just meant to be a temporary period of study. I wasn't happy with our marriage though, and I thought time away would allow me to think things through. The longer I was away, the more unhappy I realized I was. Then he threatened me with divorce if I didn't return.

I didn't realize then that according to the law of my home state I had abandoned my children because I'd left the home. It doesn't matter for how long—five months, five years, five days. And my husband took advantage of the legal situation. If I'd had good legal advice, which I didn't, I'd have known to return to the home and restore my position there before initiating the idea of divorce.

We have a son who's twelve and a daughter who's six, and I've been told now by three different lawyers, including the new lawyer I got when I came back home, that I'd lose them if I went to court. My preference would be for joint custody with my children living with me some part of the time, the time determined by the needs of the children, and that's what I'm going to try for. But I guess I didn't mind that the kids stayed with him in the sense that I felt I'd already devastated him, already taken so much away that I couldn't take them too, even if I'd been able to.

Time to Go

Sometimes the matter of where the children live is decided by a long, evolutionary process that responds both to the situations of the parents at different times and to the changing needs of the children.

We were married three years, and at the time my husband left we had two sons, the youngest just over a year old. My husband was always very good with the children. I had rather mixed feelings about motherhood. Some parts of it I liked, some I didn't. But during our marriage we stuck to typical sex roles. I worked and did evey-thing at home too. That was just taken for granted At the time he left, the women's movement and consciousness raising and all that stuff was in the air. I began immediately to work full time. I really wanted to. And then I had moments of regretting my motherhood.

At the end of our marriage my husband had begun to drink alco-holically, but after we'd been separated about a year he was getting himself together. He was involved with a woman who had a daugh-ter. I'd been working and taking care of the kids and finding that draining, so we decided together, with a therapist, that I probably could use a rest and that he should take the kids for a while. I thought that was the most generous thing to do, and it solved everybody's problems, and I liked the idea that my kids would be involved with a little family group. That was more than I could give them.

But within a few months he took a job down South and went alone, leaving the children with his mother. So I went and got them. They were two and four at that point. And during the period after I took them back I began to feel the joy of being a mother. I really enjoyed it. All along my husband continued to want the children, but he also continued to have trouble with alcohol, so he just wasn't capable of taking them.

Then a few years ago he got sober and seemed quite solid; he was seeing the kids regularly. He was involved with a woman who was very good with the kids. And in the back of my mind I began to think that maybe in a few years he'd take them full time. I had a lot of pressures. I was holding down two jobs and working like a horse, but I still couldn't give them much. We still came out poor. And my age was pressing on me, how long could I wait to start to really develop myself?

I went away for five weeks one summer and left the kids with him, and when I cam back my oldest son said he really wanted to stay with his father. Then I had to begin to deal with the reality of it all. I'd been having a terrible time with this child. He was heading into his teens and starting to rebel. So I thought okay, he can stay, but the youngest must be with me. And he was for the next six months. But when his brother came to visit on the weekends they'd have awful fights, and I saw that the situation, the way it was set up, made it seem that their father was accepting the older one and rejecting the younger. I realized they should be together. Also I was at a point where I just couldn't manage anymore.

So I went to their father and I said, "Okay, I'm tired. I want my own life. And having one of the kids is just as much of a burden as having two. It still doesn't leave me with any time. It's also bad for the boys to be split up. It's not doing anything for them." I wish I could have let them both go at once. I worry now that my older son will think I let him go too easily.

They've been with their father for two years now, and it's been great for them. The older one is like a changed person; the younger one seems very secure. And I'm very satisfied with the situation. But I was quite passive about making the decision. If my husband hadn't kept knocking on the door I might just have gone on with things the way they were, and that wouldn't have been good for any of us.

"Kidnapping"?

One of the most painful and traumatic ways of effecting a custody arrangement occurs when one parent seizes the children from the other. This leaves particularly vivid scars on everyone involved.

Even when the end result proves beneficial, the action that brought about the situation leaves its unpleasant marks.

At the time of our divorce our kids were ten and seven, and I automatically assumed they'd live with me. My husband felt he wanted them, but he didn't object to my having them. When we'd been divorced three years they were visiting him one weekend, and I got a message on my answering machine saying they wouldn't be coming home, ever again. When I heard that I almost flipped out. I couldn't believe it. I called him and said, "You can't do that." He said he could and he would. I asked to speak to them, and he wouldn't let me.

When I went there a few weeks later, he wouldn't even let me take them out of the house. He was fearful that I'd try to kidnap them back. I had to take them into their bedrooms to talk privately to them. That was probably the heaviest time of my life. I asked what they wanted, where they'd be happier, what their feelings were. What was painful was when I heard them say they'd rather live with their father, for various reasons. The divorce had been very rough on them; they'd never really gotten over it. My ex-husband had remarried, and they felt being in a family unit would make them happier. He lived in suburbia where they'd grown up. They had never really adjusted to living with me in the city. They also felt he could give them more materially. I certainly wasn't financially secure. We had to work to make ends meet when they were with me.

So I had to make a decision. A lot of this period of time I block. I don't even remember it it was so painful. This was the hardest decision I ever had to make, and I don't know how long it took me—months, I guess. I was in therapy at the time, thank God. I felt everything my kids had said was true, and, in addition, my daughter and I had been having terrible problems with each other. She blamed me for the divorce and resented it. There was a lot of bitterness and anger. But their emotional health was a tremendous concern to me, and I knew he couldn't give them that. That was the problem in our marriage: there was no communication. You couldn't talk to him. But I kept telling myself that I'd already given them the nonmaterial things. They already had a basis. So I decided to let them go, not to contest it, and hope that they'd still come to me when they needed me for things that were important.

I guess I could have given their living with him a trial period rather than giving up custody, but I just couldn't battle in court with him. I wanted it settled. I really believe that what I did was totally unselfish. If I'd known what I was going to go through, I wonder how unselfish I would have been. But now I'm getting a grip on my life, and I like it this way. Now I have the freedom and time to get what I want out of my own life.

A Sense of Victimhood

The climate of our culture being what it is, it is extremely difficult for some women to acknowledge their needs, even to themselves, if those needs are at odds with cultural notions of what they should be. Their need may be to live apart from their children but making an overt choice to do so would be wholly unacceptable. Instead, such women arrange to be victimized in one way or another. They manipulate the custody situation, consciously or unconsciously, so that they will end up without their children, which may be what they wanted all along but found impossible to face. They arrange to "lose" their children.

For some women it is easier to believe almost anything—that they are too unstable to have their kids, that the children's father took them away, that they are cursed by bad luck, bad breaks—than to believe that they would voluntarily part with their children. Almost any alternative seems more socially acceptable than that. These are the women who have the hardest time accepting and recovering from the separation from their children. Women who are able to be honest about their needs and motives, and to take responsibility for them, tend to experience the choice of living without their children as a positive one, whatever its attendant pain. Women who use a kind of victimhood as the vehicle by which they part from their children tend to have a hard time shaking that off. Their sense of themselves as victims seeps into all areas of their lives, and they often seem unable to move beyond it.

Very often the theme in these women's stories is *if only*. If only I had had better lawyers, more money, more help; if only my husband were less powerful, less vindictive, more magnanimous; if only we had lived some place else, had different lives; if only, if only. While it may seem evident to us that once these women are without their children they have achieved, albeit inadvertently, a desired goal, it is very difficult for them to reap any positive benefits—believing as they do that something awful has been done to them.

My husband came to me one day and said he couldn't stand it anymore, and I said I couldn't either, and he said could he call a lawyer, and I said yes. It was understood that he wanted the children. He'd been adopted himself, and he always knew he wasn't letting go of his kids. In that way I guess he thought he could redress what had happened to him. I wanted the children, but I knew I couldn't negotiate with him. I felt really helpless. He and his mother lined up against me. What a team! I fought for the children, but it was hopeless—my jerk lawyer against their three. I had nothing to fight with. I don't see that I had a choice. I don't go with voices who say you can influence what happens. Want? *Whether I* wanted *the children or not didn't have anything to do with it.*

When I left it was a necessity for me. But even if I got a good lawyer there wasn't going to be much hope for me about getting the kids. My husband knows every judge in the county.

I made some bad mistakes and I had bad luck, and the great irony is that every time I try to do something that's best for my son, at great expense to myself, it backfires. We have a trial pending. My husband wants custody and says our son wants to live with him. They say that the fact I allowed the child to go live with his father for three months, when I 'd been very sick, means that I abandoned him. Also, I signed something I shouldn't have, saying he could stay with his father until June of this year when I really meant to say June of last yar. They're using that. And all of this is back and forth between two countries. I don't have a job. I'm ten thousand dollars in debt. How can I pay to get my witnesses to a trial? I can't pay to see a therapist. I'm just trying very hard not to fall apart.

During our marriage my ex traveled a great deal, and I was being torn to pieces with two infant children. When they were six and eight a lawyer suggested sending them to a boarding school, and I did that. After we separated I moved into the city and got a full-time job. My ex remarried and started custody proceedings. I think he thought custody would be cheaper than paying child support. It was a terrible time—he's a very hostile man, very angry. I won the proceedings in court and got custody in August.

Then I sent them back to school that fall. I was worn out. I just wanted them in school for that year, and then I'd decide what to do. But then their boarding school closed and here they were with me, and I had a full-time job. My ex started custody proceedings again, and I lost my job because the head of the school where I worked didn't want the name of the school used in court. My lawyer said she wouldn't help me in a second custody fight. She said I should give the children to him so they wouldn't be dragged into all this again. It never occurred to me that we could have joint custody. So they went. I remember the night very well.

I couldn't see them very much after that beacuse I was sick, and it took about two-and-a-half years for my physical problems to clear up. Then one Sunday I went to call the children, and the operator said the number was discontinued and there was no forwarding number. I thought I'd die. They'd just disappeared.

Well, I've gone through sixty thousand dollars trying to find them. I'm cleaned out, wiped out at age fifty-three. But I fianlly found them out West, and now I'm allowed to see them four times a year, although I can't afford the air fare. He wanted to give them to me in court, right now, take them two days from now, he said. I couldn't just yank them out of school. I have a studio apartment that wouldn't be big enough. My daughter needs therapy, which I couldn't afford. I don't think I'll ever get over giving them to him.

We'd been living overseas, and at the end of our marriage I left without my husband knowing. I just packed up lock, stock and barrel, and children and came back to the United States because I was afraid if I stayed over there he'd get the children. I had no means of support, no place to go there. I'd tried to get help, but I was afraid to confide in many people for fear they'd go back to him. My options were really cut, and I got no help from any of the people I approached. I had no money for real legal advice, and I thought the best thing was to get the hell out of there, which is what I did.

I had the children living with me for about a year and a half, and then at one point he came to this country and just took them off the streets and took them back overseas with him. There had been no legal custody decision so he had as much right to them as I had. So then the whole question arose of what did I really want. I had a talk with my mother one day—the moment is so clear to me. She was so frustrated because we didn't really communicate very well, and she finally said, "I don't understand. These are your children. It's not natural for them to be apart from you. Don't you want them?" And I couldn't even say to myself no, I don't, *even though the way we had been living was so difficult for me.*

My kids' father hadn't been there to come to take them on weekends or once a week overnight. I had full responsibility, and he didn't give us a nickel, and I was on welfare and trying to get into college so I could get a decent job. And welfare was hassling me because you're not allowed to go to school. I wasn't living in a very comfortable apartment, and my kids had lived so much better when we were with their father.

So when they went I was partly relieved. I had a wonderful time. I didn't have to worry and make arrangements about baby-sitters or get up in time to make sure they got to school or make their lunches. I saw a whole other side of living. I was an adult on my own for the first time in my life. I had my own place to live. I could come and go or never come home, and no one would ask me why. So it was very hard for me to understand what I was doing. I couldn't just say this is what I really want.

After a few months I went overseas to be near them and to try to do something, but it was just an uphill battle and nothing really worked. He had the money, he had the connections, he had the children, he had the house, and he had a business. It was just very difficult. My whole life was influenced by money or the lack of it. If I'd had more money I would have had more help, better lawyers. If my children wanted to be with me now I couldn't imagine it financially. I don't have a big enough apartment nor could I afford to get one. I couldn't afford to send them to private schools. I don't have a circle of friends that would include other parents. I wouldn't have anything to offer my children if they lived with me.

So many things are evident in this last story that seem typical of the women who have difficulty being candid with themselves regarding their children and custody: a lack of self-awareness, a feeling of obligation to go through the motions of a fight for the children, an inability to acknowledge one's own needs and desires, a continuing sense of impoverishment, a feeling of loss of control, a feeling of helplessness. Their need to hide, even from themselves, their true needs and desires is a telling index of how disapproving our society's attitude is toward noncustodial mothers.

FOUR

The Response

One of the things that makes a woman's decision to live apart from her children so difficult is that she is often operating in a vacuum while she is making it. Very few of the women we interviewed knew anyone else who had made such a choice. Adding to the sense of isolation was the lack of support or understanding these women encountered. Frequently they were met, as one woman put it, by "judgments, not kindness." And the recriminations were just as likely to come from families and friends as from strangers. It is apparently disconcerting to nearly everyone when a mother steps outside the traditional definition of her role.

Parental Disapproval

Sometimes the most hostile reaction to a woman making this choice comes from her own mother. Few statements in our workshops met with such murmurs of assent as those about a woman's mother being her biggest problem. In the first workshop we held on this issue one woman remarked, "I'd be doing fine with this if it weren't for my mother," and sounds of agreement came from almost every woman in the room.

This hostility may arise from a mother's resenting her daughter's exercising an option the mother never felt *she* had. It might come from a sense that her daughter's action reflects poorly on the mother's own parenting ability. Who, after all, was the daughter's model for motherhood? Whatever the reason, this reaction, when it comes, is especially disturbing.

My mother completely disassociated herself from me during this. She didn't want to hear anything. She said her nerves were too bad, whatever that means. And now, even though I've sent my kids into a loving situation, she accuses me of being a terrible mother. She was the one who was a terrible mother. My growing up was horrible.

My mother was the only one who said to me, "How can you do this? I don't understand."

My family was beside themselves over this, so horribly unhappy. They couldn't understand what I was doing. They felt I'd betrayed them. My mother, at the beginning, sided with my ex-husband. Only recently she said to me, "I was never really behind you, but I am now."

I've had a lot of problems about my decision about the children, and they mostly come from my mother. Sometimes she goes overboard to overcompensate and tells me I'm a pioneer. But then she'll call me first thing in the morning and tell me my daughter just called her to say she needs to be picked up from school. And the message is that my daughter's being neglected, that no one's looking after her. Or she'll tell me I should be in court fighting for custody. We have joint custody now. A couple of weeks ago, in fact, I went back to see my therapist because I was beginning again to see myself as a terrible person after it taking two-and-a-half years in therapy to make me believe I wasn't a terrible person. I could see myself slipping back, having dreams at night about my abandoned children. And that all comes from my mother. I haven't really had too much social pressure, but she undermines my self-esteem. She can really do a job on me.

No one can make me feel as bad about this as my mother. She has two responses to it. One is badgering me . How could I? What will people think? What am I *thinking? The other is being silent and looking hurt and sort of desperate. Either one of these makes me feel pretty terrible.*

Occasionally, it is the father who is more outspoken in his disapproval.

My parents' response to this was terrible. My father took me to lunch and told me my first duty as a married woman was to my husband and my second duty was to my children and that I was foregoing all the good things in life. The world was tough, he said, and what did I expect to make of myself in it? I said I would listen to what he had to say, but then I would make my own decisions. He was quite upset and didn't want to talk to me for a while, so I just kept away. He was angry that I wouldn't behave like a good little child.

My father has completely disowned me over this whole thing. He says I belong with my children, and he refuses to talk to me. My mother, on the other hand, says she doesn't necessarily agree with me but she loves me because I'm her daughter.

Sometimes the family is united in condemnation.

My parents' attitude is disgust. What kind of mother would give up her children? She must be crazy.

I have a sixteen-year-old son who just went to live with his father, and my biggest problem is really my parents. Every day they ask, "Why have you failed?"

I didn't really have any support from anyone for this decision. My parents thought I was crazy. The family didn't think I could do it. My mother's flipping out over this. My brother yells at me for upsetting the whole family. My father, as a matter of fact, still thinks I could get my son back anytime I want. No one wants to confront him to tell him what has really happened.

My mother and father feel I failed them. They take my divorce, my son living with his father as their failure. I'm just not doing things the way they think I should. And they keep feeding me guilt. They're very much against this arrangement.

My parents were heartbroken when I left the kids. They couldn't understand how I could do it. Their disapproval was under the surface, but it was there.

My parents were upset, very upset. I think my mother thought I was out of touch with reality, that I had a problem and that I should get help for it. My father eventually said, "You have to do what's best for you." My sisters didn't understand because they had happy marriages and were loving motherhood. They said they could never do such a thing and they didn't know how I could, but I was doing it, so okay.

First my parents urged me to call my husband's bluff and let him try dealing with the kids since he said he wanted them. But then when it worked out and the kids didn't come back to me, my parents told me what a terrible person I was, what a terrible mother.

For a long time I felt sorry for myself that both my parents were dead. But now, in this situation, I think maybe I'm the lucky one. There's less guilt for me. There's no one to say how could you? How could you leave your children?

What Others Think

Parents and families aren't the only ones who ask such questions and who render such judgments. Hostile responses come from friends and acquaintances as well.

The hardest thing to deal with was people's reactions—the unspoken word, the look, saying how could you possibly do what you've done?

I'm not sure if I had guilt feelings because I allowed people to make me feel guilty or if the guilt was really there. What I am sure of is that no one stood by us in the family. I was completely alienated. Even so-called friends, who weren't really, wouldn't speak to me. This was ten years ago, but if I still lived in that town now I'd still be getting flak. People would still be turning their backs and not speaking. It's a little easier for me to talk about it here at the other end of the country.

I was aware of the kind of withdrawal I'd get from people when I'd explain my situation, the kind of intake of breath, the awkwardness, the sense that they were thinking: "What do I say now?" Even though I didn't personally experience a lot of stigmatization, I was aware that it was there. A friend of mine who I'd thought was very supportive confessed to me some months later that when he heard I'd left my children with my husband, he thought there was something wrong with me.

People consider me somewhat of a freak when they hear I've left my five children. I get that sort of raised-eyebrow reaction that says what kind of woman are you? How could you do it? You've got a baby? But sometimes if I really want to take the time I'll explain to them that I felt better leaving the children as a family, that I thought the divorce would be upsetting enough, that the two oldest didn't want to come with me, and I wasn't going to split the kids up. After that there aren't too many raised eyebrows. But a man would never get this response in the first place. He'd never feel compelled to explain.

People reacted with gasps. No magazine printed articles about this; there were no books in the library. I remember a friend saying to me I must be one of the first people to do this.

Most of my friends completely deserted me. One or two close friends stuck with me, and I wouldn't have made it without them. They agreed my decision was the best way in the circumstances. Some time earlier I'd heard that an old friend of mine had left her husband and given him custody, and I was shocked. I thought how can a woman do that? Now I understand.

My closest friend was supportive, but on some level I was unsure of people's reactions and fearful of them. There were plenty of times when people didn't understand.

You feel things from people even when they don't say much. And that made me feel bad, guilty; there's some shame attached to it. I felt embarrassed. Even when I lived in India I didn't talk about it because I feared other people's reactions.

I did this in 1975, and the only people I got support from were the artistic people in the community, and of course they were considered the freaks. Mostly I've gotten negative responses to my decision, but that didn't surprise me. I stopped looking to other people for feedback because I got so little support when I was a twenty-five-year-old divorcee trying to raise three children. I guess what I'm trying to say is that I didn't have any expectation of support for my decision.

Exceptions to the Rule

There are, of course, also instances in which families and friends offer support to women in this situation rather than heaping negative judgments upon them. But these seemed to be the exception rather than the rule.

Both my parents were very supportive. They knew how bad things were in my marriage. I was surprised though by their ability to accept this. It was so alien to their way of thinking. And most of my friends were supportive too.

When I was trying to make my decision I did speak to my parents about it, and they were, surprisingly enough, very supportive of it. They felt that it was a tremendous responsibility for me to continue to have the kids by myself and that I should let the kids go and have a life for myself. The kids would be taken care of. Their father's not a bad person. My parents kept saying, "It's now your time. Take your freedom." They're in their seventies, and never had I anticipated that they'd be behind me. That gave me strength. Also I had an aunt who supported me. But I didn't talk to friends. I was a little embarrassed, and I felt guilty. I felt they wouldn't understand.

My parents' first concern was for the children, but when I made a firm decision they went along with it and were very supportive. My closest friends were not surprised and were very supportive. Neighbors and acquaintances were absolutely shocked. Nobody could understand. At the time I'd gone through so much thinking and agonizing that those reactions just weren't a factor. I simply tuned them out. Family reactions were very significant to me though, and I'm still constantly internally justifying myself to my husband's family. I con-

tinue to imagine what they think and what they say. But I think basically if you are comfortable in your decision, no matter how unusual it is, I think everybody else will in time go along with you.

The Price One Pays

Another reaction these women sometimes have to contend with is a sour-grapes mixture of envy and resentment from women who are living with their children. A participant in one of our workshops reported that she had felt other women were jealous of her escape from the daily grind of full-time motherhood. Other members of the workshop agreed that they too had encountered this response.

But perhaps no group of people is as hard on these women as they are on themselves. Their inner responses to the decision they have made are in many cases every bit as stringent as those they receive from the outside world. The nasty questions they hear, or sense, from other people are the same ones they are likely to ask themselves. Making this choice necessitates setting aside a lifetime of conditioning, and few women are able to do that without a great deal of guilt and ambivalance and fear. Even those women who manage to avoid the ambivalance and fear, and there are a few, seldom escape the guilt as well. That's the price they pay for so thoroughly enjoying their new situation.

I went through hell for a year, real torture and depression. And when I was depressed I'd feel total rejection from my kids. I personalized it, feeling they preferred their father to me, which was absurd. The horrible aftermath for me was partly the guilt. Did I do the right thing? How could a mother do this? Another part was loneliness. I'd always been with my kids, and it came very naturally to me to be a mother. At one point I had a plant shop in my home so I was with them even when I was working. I really only had brief glimpses of anything positive at the time I let them go. How could I even know what that would be like? Now I think being just me is wonderful, but then I couldn't imagine my future without them. I didn't think of it, of me. I just tried to figure what would be best for them. Now I wouldn't want them to live with me. I'm getting a grip on my own life, and I want it this way now.

The beginning was very difficult. I was thirty-four years old and I'd never lived alone. The silence was deafening. When I was considering having my kids live with their father I felt I would like the greater freedom I had without them, but I wouldn't have told anyone that—those were the feelings I'd harbor and feel guilty about.

I don't know if I've developed a selfish streak or what, but all of a sudden I realize I like my life-style the way it is. I really don't think at this point that I could ever take the children back. And now my problem is guilt. I never could understand how fathers without custody would skip weekend visitations, but I do now. Every once in awhile I'll skip a weekend and go skiing or something, and then I'll feel guilty because I don't feel guilty.

I had a lot of guilt when my kids left even though I consider my ex-husband a very good father. I wanted my own life and that was bad. I also felt guilty that I'd never given them all they should have had. But now I feel like I've been born again. I feel like I just got out of high school and I have a chance to learn things about myself that I didn't know. I'm like a teenager.

I felt I'd been there in my son's formative years. He's fifteen years old now, and I raised him. But I still fear he'll wake up one morning and hate me—that's constant. I have some positive feelings but they're accompanied by guilt. I know my life is much better now that I'm out of my marriage and, other than my son, I feel I'm the luckiest woman in the world. I have a chance to live my life again, a second chance. But my guilt is worst at those times when I forget I have a son. That's the worst.

I was concerned for my daughter, worried. I'm sure I felt I'd failed. Her father's attitudes toward children were very different from mine, so I was apprehensive about that. He doesn't coddle his children, and he doesn't show too much affection, and that never made me happy. But he's a less nervous parent than I am, and that was positive. And she wanted to go with him. Still, I felt guilty.

If I think of my own mother doing that to me, I think it's the most horrible thing in the world. How could I do that to my own children? That's how I think when I'm feeling particularly down. But rationally, intellectually, I think it's an okay decision. I think they're probably better off with their father than if they'd moved with me to some apartment and I was screaming and yelling all the time. I don't know. I don't see why a father can't be as good a parent as a mother. But that's objective, and it doesn't always sit right when you're going through it. Sometimes it hurts like hell, sometimes I'm fine.

I felt positive about the decision, but at first I just felt really guilty because I didn't miss my son. Now I feel guilty that other people will think badly of me for being in this situation.

My mother always felt badly that I'm not as maternal as she thinks I should be or as she was. And I feel guilty about that but also a little angry. I shouldn't have to defend myself. But then sometimes I think she's right. I used to feel stronger inside myself than I do now. Now when someone makes a judgment about me I halfway believe them.

When a woman steps out of the role of full-time mother, she lets go of a large piece of herself, a piece she may have been using to conceal other things.

For the first year without my son living with me I was euphoric. It was wonderful to be without that responsibility for the first time. I'd always worked, but even that was different without the responsibility of him. I felt relieved, free as a bird. Now things were churning around more. I realize my son was a scapegoat for lots of my problems. If I had not had him I would have done this, I would have done that. But now he's not here, and I still don't do this and do that. I no longer have the excuse of him, and it's made me a lot more clear about myself.

I know I was putting myself on the line as far as a career went. Now I had all the time and freedom in the world, nothing to hide behind. It took courage to let go of the idea of being a mother. Okay, I said to myself, you believe in yourself? Prove it. Go for it.

I certainly hid behind my kids. With me, whenever things weren't going right, I'd have another child because I loved having them. I loved taking care of them. I loved being home and playing house, growing up with them. And whenever I got bored, it was just time to have another. Well, now all that has changed. Without them, I feel much more exposed somehow.

For years I'd thought, and expressed to friends, that the reason I hadn't really become something was because I had the responsibility for these children. Now I didn't have the excuse, and I wondered if I'd have the talent, the intelligence, the motivation to act. I didn't even really know I was hiding behind the children, until they were gone.

Feeling the Loss

For some women the primary feeling in the aftermath of the decision is an acute sense of loss. Their assessment of the decision itself—positive, negative, ambivalent—seemed irrelevant to whether or not they experienced this response.

I feel the loss of him. I didn't know how strong the maternal instinct was until he left. It's a true physical need. I sometimes just need to hug him. I combat this sense of loss by swimming, jogging, keeping very busy. Otherwise I'd go a little crackers.

Sometimes the feeling of separation and isolation is torture, absolute hell. I get a real hunger for my kids, a real physical need for them.

After the kids left I sort of collapsed. Nothing happened outwardly really, but I just felt I was missing a part of myself. I felt an incredible sense of loss as though part of my body was missing.

The first six months went pretty well. I was very excited by my new life, by my sudden autonomy, by my not having to account to anybody for anything. I was exhilarated. I didn't feel guilt. I didn't feel much pain. But gradually, as time passed, I also had a growing awareness of my own pain, a true realization of the loss I was suffering. I had no doubts about what I was doing, but I finally began letting in the pain that I felt at the ending of a certain relationship with my kids.

Suffering Rejection

One of the greatest concerns for these women is how their children will respond to their decision. They know that the culture in general views their behavior as rejecting, and they fear, no matter how they handle it, that their children will see it that way as well.

When I told my son what I was going to do, he was so angry. He just stopped talking to me. I knew he hated me for what I was doing—breaking up his home—and I didn't blame him. Finally I got him to tell me what he felt, and I cried, pretty hysterically, I'm afraid. Then I told him, "You have to understand. I'm not abandoning you. I'm leaving you with your father. And there's a big difference." We really had it out then, and after that things got better.

When my kids ask me why I'm not living in their town anymore I say, "I'm not happy there. I'm not happy with your father. I'm not happy in that town." I don't know how much they understand, but you have to give some answer when they ask questions like that, and it should be the truth. It is very hard though to explain to a child that in a certain area there's no social life or no work or whatever. The child thinks, Well, I'm here. Isn't that enough?

My children wanted to go with their father, but it was still an adjustment and a change for them. Initially there was a lot of fighting between the two of them. When I'd pick them up for a weekend they'd have to warm up to me again, and there was a lot of competition for my attention. But now I think they've adjusted pretty well. There was a time though when my son wanted to come back to live with me, and he did for a short time, but then he ended up back with his father.

When he decided he wanted to move back in with me it was all very sudden. He just had *to do it right then, and it was a very intense work period for me. I had a lot of people at the house, meetings going on all the time. Things were really crackling around here. And*

I felt a little guilty because I really didn't have much time for him. I was working morning, noon, and night. He said it was fine, that he understood, but he was feeling ignored. I could tell that and I felt badly about it. But the situation just really wasn't right for either one of us at that point.

My son asked me why I don't live closer so we can see each other more, and I could only say, "I don't have an answer for you." And I don't. I only know when he asked why I couldn't be there that I felt like shit.

Even if the child wants *to go to the father, I think it's important to explain this move in terms of it really being best for both of you. I didn't do that, and my son has expressed guilt about leaving me. He feels he left me alone.*

When people say, "Oh, my children are sailing through this so beautifully," it probably means the kids are repressing and their response will come out when they're twenty-five or fifty or in six months, a year, two years. My son started fighting in school during the second year, not the first. He started having fights in the playground. Now he's not fighting anymore. So that's what he had to do, and it's not the worst thing in the world. Kids absolutely will respond, but they may not respond at the moment that things are happening. It may come up later.

Reflections in Kind

Few parents can separate from a child easily. Distress, a kind of anguish, are almost always built into the act. But there are parents, some of them mothers, who make that move with a certain sense of confidence and self-possession, persuaded that it is the right one for everybody concerned. Such women report not only their own positive feelings but a generally positive response from other people as well. Their assurance, their conviction, seem to ease the way along this difficult path. Apparently, the way a woman feels about her own behavior may be reflected back to her in kind.

I've never had much problem with people's responses. I find that if you explain it to people in a positive way they back off. If I were insecure about it and looking for reassurance, then I'd be opening myself to criticism but I've never done that. I've always felt that it was the right thing to do. And I think I've made it clear that I wouldn't deal with a lot of flak about it.

All my friends were supportive. I had no feelings of guilt about this. I felt some trepidation about being alone for the first time in my life, but I certainly didn't feel I was losing my kids. Quite the opposite. And now I've discovered that I love my aloneness. When I was married I could never be alone. I always had insomnia during my marriage because lying in bed at night was the only time when I could be alone and think. I haven't had one night of insomnia since I've been living by myself.

I discussed all this with my attorney before approaching my husband. He said, "If you're leaving your children I want you to be totally prepared emotionally for what you're doing. Be clear about how you really feel. I'd like you to see a therapist to make sure you know how you feel." And I did go to a therapist for nearly a year.

I had loved being a mother. It was a wonderful experience. And I didn't feel overburdened by my children. I didn't feel that I wanted to escape from them. But work was very important to me, a real ego booster. I was afraid I'd be very lonely, but I wasn't afraid to leave. I felt I was going to make it. And I felt that my husband was going to make it too. And that the kids would be fine.

I haven't been ostracized or treated like a leper by people when they hear I'm not living with my kids. I guess it's how you feel about yourself that creates other people's reactions, and I felt I was doing the right thing. I didn't feel guilty because my kids seemed so comfortable with it. It was wrenching to move out, but I had no guilt about it. My younger son had been depressed the last few years of the marriage. If we took him to a movie with a happy ending he'd complain about it. "Nothing in life ends happily," he'd say. But one day recently he said to me, "Oh, Mommy, life is so wonderful." And I felt so good. I felt I'd done the right thing.

FIVE

Part-time Mother

I feel such a sense of isolation from my children! You can make all the appointments in the world, lunches, dinners, movies, sleepovers, what have you, but it doesn't make up for the fact that you don't brush shoulders with them on the way into the bathroom or the kitchen. I love being able to eat what I want when I want. I turned my dining room into a den and I love eating on my lap. But I miss that daily connection with my kids. I don't want my daughter to come to me and say, "Will you type my paper on the women's movement?" I want to see the index cards all over the floor. I want to see that paper being put together. I do know I'm the only one who gives her undivided attention. I miss the day-to-day contact. I feel like a caring aunt, not a mother. And I also feel guilty because it's so pleasant not to have the day-to-day responsibilities of being a mother.

The Visiting-Parent Role

This woman vividly conveys the essence of part-time motherhood as so many women experience it: the regret about moving to the periphery of their children's lives, the guilt, and yet the enjoyment of a new kind of freedom. Many aspects of part-time parenthood are the same for women as they are for men who have become noncustodial fathers. Certain things go with the role of visiting parent no matter what the sex of that parent.

One is the practical problem of the logistics and mechanics of visiting: the time and place of visits, number of children to be visited with at one time, how to spend the visitation time, and so on. Another is getting used to the limits of the new role of visiting parent: How much influence do visiting parents now have in their children's lives? Can they discipline them? Do they still help out with homework? What is proper input and what isn't? What constitutes involvement in the children's lives but stops short of interference in the full-time parent's sphere?

Another experience common to visiting parents of both sexes is that of dealing with an ex-spouse's remarriage and the fact that one's children are now being raised by someone else. Still another is the problem of communication with one's ex-mate, how to keep the channels open for the good of the child. Both noncustodial mothers and fathers experience frustration when they have substantial differences with their ex-spouses on child-rearing matters. At times, both find it painful to see in their children reflections of their ex-mate, a mate with whom, after all, they were unable to live. And both men and women, when they assume the visiting-parent role, find it tempting to play Santa Claus with their children, although a woman's economic situation is apt to make this less likely.

But while there are similarities between noncustodial mothers and fathers, there are also marked differences. Since a mother has usually been the primary caretaker, the leap from that role to that of visiting parent is a larger one than that essayed by a traditional father separating from his children. And the adjustment to the new role is correspondingly greater.

Learning to Say Good-bye

We do not mean to imply that it is easy for a father to live apart from his children. Fathers in this position certainly suffer the feelings of loneliness and isolation that accompany moving out of a family-living arrangement. Fathers also may feel the guilt that stems from a sense of personal failure at having a marriage end. It is no easier for a father to say good-bye to his children at the close of a visit than it is for a mother.

But a mother living apart from her children has all those feelings *plus* the additional burden of being on the receiving end of some quite severe judgments, which are great producers of guilt. And guilt can be particularly destructive when wedded to the visiting-parent role. One thing it can do is to cause visits to diminish. A mother who is feeling guilty about the course she has chosen may begin to perceive her children as painful reminders of that guilt and decrease her visits so as not to be reminded. That decrease, of course, only amplifies the guilt, and a cycle is established that can lead to a mother's withdrawing from her children altogether.

> *I had a really hard time seeing my kids in the year after the divorce. I thought I'd probably made the right decision, but I felt very guilty about it. I knew it wasn't what a mother was supposed to do, even though I couldn't see any other way. My ex-husband never made anything any easier. He was constantly fighting me about visitation. I'd go to pick the kids up and they wouldn't be there. And it was hard to listen to them cry about how their father yelled at me on the phone. Also, I never knew when they would reject me.*
>
> *I remember one day vividly. I went to pick them up and they were ready to go, and they got in the car and then they popped back out and said, "Mom, we don't want to go with you. We want to be in the bicycle parade." Well, I was devastated. It was just so hard living in the same community with them and having all these feelings. It seemed like it would be easier to leave altogether, so I moved out of the state, across the country, and that's made it hard to keep in touch with my kids. I've only seen them once in the last ten years.*

> *I knew I couldn't have survived if I kept my kids after the divorce. I just couldn't handle them and I knew it. I couldn't handle much of anything at that point. So I felt it was right that they be with their father, and he certainly wanted them. That wasn't ever in doubt. But none of that stopped me from feeling horribly guilty about it. I don't think there's anything worse in people's eyes—maybe a murderer or a rapist—than a mother who leaves her children. And I absolutely bought into that. I knew there was a special place reserved in hell*

for me. I was sure of it. And seeing my kids only seemed to reinforce the most negative feelings I had. I'd just look at them and plunge right into the abyss. So I suppose to avoid that feeling I began to avoid seeing them. I started staying away, making excuses, and then finally I moved away and stayed away for a few years.

Now I live near them again, and we're trying to reestablish some sort of relationship, but it's hard. I was out of contact with them for a while, and you can't just walk back into their lives and pick up where you left off. I wish I hadn't withdrawn the way I did, but at the time it seemed like the only thing I could do.

Guilty Pleasure

Part-time mothers suffer from another sort of guilt as well. Some of the women we talked with reported that their worst guilt occurred at those times when they were taking the most pleasure in their new situation.

I was guilty because I wasn't really guilty, do you know what I mean? I was supposed to be guilty because I was doing this terrible thing, but I didn't really feel that. I felt relieved and free and lighter than I'd felt in years. For a long time during my marriage I felt fat and sloppy, and it was hard for me to drag myself around. Well, I don't weigh any less now, but I don't feel that heaviness anymore. The only responsibility I had suddenly was to myself, and I loved that. That seemed just great. But as soon as I let myself know how terrific I felt about it, then the guilt set in.

I remember the first few months I was living apart from the kids. I'd come home from work at night and just sit down and do nothing sometimes and think how miraculous that was—to just sit there and do nothing and have nobody demanding that I do anything. That was the most incredible feeling. It was wonderful. But of course it felt sinful too. I didn't feel I should be enjoying myself so much.

Living at a Remove

A mother living apart from her children has moved from a role embodying almost total control to a role that very often seems to involve no control at all. She has been intimately involved with the comings and goings of her children's daily lives, with their moods, their meals, the minute details of school and friendships, their likes and dislikes, their fears and joys. Now, quite suddenly, she is at one remove, seeing the children at prescribed times, often in a place unfamiliar to them. Someone else is now in charge of their daily lives, making decisions about the hours they keep, dentist appointments and back-to-school shopping, influencing in a very powerful way their ideas and attitudes. For a woman to make the transition from the former position to the latter can be extremely difficult.

It seems so strange to me that for fifteen years I was involved in every aspect of his life, and now he goes to a school I've never even seen. That frightens me sometimes. He lives in the Midwest now, and I'm in the East, and it's hard to know how to keep in touch with his life and at the same time not disrupt it.

I guess when the kids were living with me and I was into meditation and only allowed them to watch certain television programs and we ate a lot of peanut butter and sprouts, their father probably felt that I was ruining their lives. Now I feel that way in some respects about their life with him. There are lots of benefits to the situation, but I have a lot of trouble with some of the values he teaches them. My middle kid is already a typical American consumer person—here's what we get if we live with Mom, here's what we get if we live with Dad, so let's live with Dad because here's what we're gonna get. We can always have Mom. Mom will always be Mom. He just lays it right out, that simple. And I realize that all I can do is just concentrate on myself and trust that some other seeds were planted in whatever time I had with them.

I was very close to my daughters when I was living with them, but now I don't feel that I have any impact on their growing up, on their character.

I've learned that I have very little control over molding and shaping their attitudes, their personalities, their values. They're so much more an extension of the spouse you don't like. There were things I liked in my kids that I've seen change since they lived with father.

My ex-husband and I have joint custody, and if I call him to discuss something he'll listen but he doesn't, as a rule, seek out my input, so I don't feel he's really all that interested in what I have to say. Many times he hasn't consulted me about decisions, and I think he'd be delighted if I didn't exist or at least if I lived in another part of the country. He'd be very happy to do without my input at all. A big question is where do you draw the line? When do you keep plugging your input and when do you give up.

For a few years I felt that I lost my son altogether. He was ten when he went to live with his father and stepmother. Now that he's twenty-one I see more of him, but it's clear to me that when he gets married, for instance, I'm to have nothing to do with it. I'll just be a guest. His stepmother raised him, so she'll be in charge. These are the things we just have to live with. I'll just have to accept that.

When I was visiting my son he said to me at one point, "You have no right to tell me anything. I don't need you. You don't live here." That's very hard to hear, and my instinct is to pull back, to give up, but I know I mustn't. I have to keep my hand in if I'm going to stay close to my kids. I can't withdraw no matter how much I might feel like it, no matter how tired I feel of the fray.

I don't have much influence. All I can offer my children is something that's different, a totally different way of looking at life and dealing with people. This can cause me to clash with them though, especially my daughter who's fifteen now. As she said to me, she lives with her father and his wife and she really must, for her own sanity, adopt their views on religion or feminism or sex or whatever. She must at least go along with them. And sometimes it causes her problems that I have views that are so different. It's very sad.

I have less impact on my son now, less control over him, and I sometimes feel that he tries to use my guilt to control me, to get things he wants from me. There are times when I think I should just withdraw and let him be with his father and stepmother without me hovering around. But when push comes to shove I know I'll stick it out. Why? I'm not sure why. I guess for those moments when he does need me. For instance, I wanted to be sure school was going well for him, that everything there was arranged properly. His father thinks he should automatically have the best of everything, be in the most advanced class and so on, and that isn't necessarily so. So I worked quietly on the sidelines with his guidance counselor and teachers to achieve that.

I see my son about once a month now for a weekend. He's getting older, and he's busy with all sorts of things. I miss him. I get along better with him than with anyone else in the family. I'll miss going through with him some of the wiseass, dumping on mother, teenage period.

We live far apart, and in the last couple of years I've had only sporadic contact with my son. But I think my ex-husband now realizes he's not going to get rid of me. I think he knows there's no way I'm going to drop out of the picture. He finally realizes that you can't block a mother out of her child's life. You can't just cut that bond.

Changes for the Better

Other women are quick to mention what they see as the benefits of their changed roles. Many describe an improved relationship with their children.

I go to visit my son once a month, and in a way that's nice because I don't have to discipline him. I don't have to get into day-to-day antagonisms. It makes our relationship more of a friendship. The edginess that people get when they live together isn't there.

I don't have to nag at my kids all the time. I can be the special person who comes on weekends. I bet lots of women who are with their kids all the time never talk to them the way I talk to my kids. I see lots of kids screwed up from mothers who give them their all, twenty-four hours a day.

Also, I'm giving my daughters a role model. They'll know that women can be involved in their own lives, taking responsibility for change. They'll never be victims with their lives just happening to them. They'll have the option if they don't like something to change it.

I think I'm fun for my kids now. I don't tell them what to do and what not to do. I'm not as involved in their daily lives, but that's okay. The kids are living with him. Maybe he does have better ideas about what's better for them.

When I told the children it might be a possibility that they'd go to their father, they said, "Oh good, we'll be able to do this and do that." And a voice inside me thought, Okay, go live with him, you ungrateful bastards. I've been busting my ass for you for years and this is what I get—you want to go and live with good-time Charlie. Now it's kind of fun for me to be good-time Charlie. Now they think I'm terrific, and I enjoy them more too.

But at the same time I feel a little like a grandparent. I like to see them come and visit, but boy, am I glad to see them go home. Those feelings are hard to share with most people. I feel fortunate that I have people I can tell those things to.

I think I'm much more of a romantic parent in the sense that fathers usually are. I'm an artist. I'm independent. I've made my own life. I'm not your everyday, run-of-the-mill mother that you can walk on, which is how kids generally grow up feeling about their mothers. I'm sort of special, and my daughter's a little bit in awe of me—not too much, not so much that we can't be close. For me life has been a whole lot easier because I found out real early on that I wasn't meant to be a nurturer, and now, at my daughter's present age, I'm able to be a role model and a counselor too.

For many years when I wasn't happy with the marriage, the thing which kept me from seriously considering divorce was the fact of the children. I believed children needed a stable family. Then at a certain point I came to realize that it might be better for the kids if they weren't living in a situation so tense you could cut the tension with a knife. My ex-husband and I never fought, but there was a great deal of unexpressed tension, which the kids were picking up on and acting out on. And of course that affected my relationship with them as well. But the quality of the time we have now is absolutely extraordinary. I'm able to focus on them in a way that I never could when we lived together daily. It's just wonderful, so much better than a normal relationship between parent and child.

When I was living with my kids the quality of our relationship wasn't very good. I yelled at them all the time, ordered them around. Or else I was withdrawn and didn't pay much attention. There wasn't much that was positive. Now it's very, very good, a big change for the better. Now, when they're here on the weekends, we spend really good time together.

At the time of our separation I knew I couldn't take care of my child emotionally or financially. My therapist actually said it was the right and prudent thing to do to give up custody, because he thought that emotionally I wasn't ready to take care of my son. He thought I needed a year to get my act together. And he was right—it took about a year for me to begin leading a calm, well-ordered existence. Now I see my son every other weekend, and our relationship is very, very good. I feel I betrayed him. Children have a right to parents and to a serene, secure life, and I interrupted his delicate balance. But now in the time we have together I'm capable of seeking him out, of finding out what's going on in his mind. We talk every day, and I try to make the most of the time we have.

When I lived with the children I think I treated them both like little babies. I was often irritated at my son. But my relationship is better with them now. I'm feeling better about myself than when I was in the marriage,and that makes a difference. Also I used to feel that everything I did with them was wrong because their father made me feel that way. If I bought a dress for my daughter, it was too short or too long. If I cut my son's hair, it was too short or too long. And that strain on me affected my relationship with the children. I don't have that strain now. Oh, my ex-husband tries to poison them. He tells them I'm awful. But even with all the garbage, I feel better when I'm with them. I feel more comfortable than I used to with them, and we have moments of real rapport. I think I'm much closer to my son since leaving, and I wonder if that's because my husband isn't there to interfere in our relationship.

My relationship with my son wasn't so good when I lived with him because I was crazy. I had no patience, I was unhappy, and I took it all out on him. I resented the time I spent with him. I wasn't there for him or for me. Now when I see him I'm bubbly and excited. I try to be totally with him when we're together. I let him express how he feels. I don't have to give him ultimatums anymore, although I try to teach him about the consequences of actions. When I lived with him he had to know where I was every minute. Now he can be on his own more. He's really much more secure and independent than he used to be.

Since my son has been living with his father he's more considerate, more controlled in his behavior. He can listen now, and he seems to be able to reason things out. He used to argue constantly. We seemed to work against one another. When I set up a rule he would disregard it. Also, raising him the way I was raised wasn't really good for him, but I couldn't seem to undo it. I felt very anxious about having my own life. I couldn't seem to be both a mother and woman. And I'm not even talking about having a relationship with a man. I'm just talking about the normal things a woman does outside of her children. I was constantly filled with anxiety. And I couldn't seem to work out these problems together with him. I think this separation will enable us to love one another. If we had stayed together we would have had two wrecked lives.

One of the key lessons I've learned is to love and let go. And when I let go is when I really have. I'm no longer in a hierarchical relationship to my kids where I'm above them and they have to do what I say. When I left the traditional role of director, guide, everyday parent, the relationship between me and my children became much more loving, richer, more creative. I think we have a much more truthful, honest interaction now.

Slow Growth

Sometimes it can take a number of years for a new, and better, relationship to evolve between a woman and her children.

Every time I saw my kids for ten years it was a hassle because my ex-husband would never cooperate. And I found when I saw my kids I couldn't play the role of mother to them. I was more like an aunt. But now I've realized, finally, that my kids haven't turned against me. They still love me. They confide in me. I still cry when they leave—it's another going away, another separation—but I see that I have things to give to them. I send them books I think they should be reading. They have no intellectual stimulation at home, and I can fill in that gap. I think they admire me, and last week when they came they brought a friend with them. That made me feel great.

During the marriage I never took responsibility for my son or for myself. Then, when the marriage was over, the pattern was that I would go to pick up my son and my husband would curse me out and say I was horrible, and my child would hear and not want to come with me, and I'd force him to come and we'd have a terrible time and hate each other. This went on for three years. At the end of that time he came to Florida with me for a vacation to visit my parents, but he freaked out and said he didn't want to be there so finally I sent him home, and I didn't see him then for more than a year.

During that time I began to grow up and to feel good about myself. I had been severely depressed, and I don't think I would have survived in the marriage. Eventually, I wrote a letter saying I'd like to try to have a mature relationship with my son. He has a lot of anger, but I'm able to deal with it honestly now. We see each other twice a week. I go to the house and honk the horn, and he comes out. I don't see his father; he's too negative and insulting. When my son and I are together we do whatever he likes to do. We talk a lot. We play. I help him with his schoolwork.

There seem to be several reasons that account for the improvement in mother-child relationships when the mother no longer resides with her children. Surely one is what some women describe as the welcome relief from the daily pressures of full-time motherhood. Release from complete responsibility for caretaking of the children brings with it a lessening of resentment and an increase in the energy available simply to enjoy one's children. It is relaxing to be out of the position of primary authority. "I get all the goodies and none of the crap," as one woman put it. This relief is especially welcome and healing for those women who have lived for a time as single parents and held the dual positions of caretaker and breadwinner. With the pressure off, they are able to delight in their children in ways they never thought possible.

Another factor that contributes to the decrease in tension in the mother-child relationship is the movement away from the debilitating effects of a bad marriage. Related to this, and certainly extremely important, is that these women have an improved self-image that reflects in their relationship with their children. Their self-esteem is no longer being eroded by daily involvement with the failure of their marriage. Also, the vast majority of these women are now pursuing some sort of work that they find satisfying, and that also helps to produce good feelings about themselves.

Very few of the women we talked with described a loss of self-esteem as a result of not living with their children—this despite the judgments, the guilt, the lack of support and understanding, the sometimes outright hostility their decision evoked. Most reported that, in fact, they felt better about themselves, some almost immediately, some with time. Despite all the difficulties attendant upon their decision, they felt that it ultimately enhanced, rather than diminished, them and that their children were the beneficiaries of their growth. They felt that they had more time to give to their children and that they gave it more freely than they ever had. The proposition that an unhappy parent is a poor one would not evoke much argument. But to assert that a woman may be a better parent if she is happy and living apart from her children is extremely controversial. Nevertheless, it's what many women report experiencing.

Glad to See Them Go?

Some, however, described a general lessening of parental feeling as their role in their children's lives changed.

> *When my son and I were living alone the quality of our relationship was really good. I was in school so I didn't spend all that much time with him, but I really enjoyed him when I did. It was just us and it was really nice. Now I love him, but he's a seven-year-old boy, and he's into all this seven-year-old boy stuff and I'm really not. His father plays with him. I just don't. I feel like he has his own life*

that's apart from me. My role in his life has become sort of peripheral, but that doesn't really bother me.

It makes me sad that my relationship with my son didn't turn out to be what I thought it would be when I was younger. I thought I'd have the communication with him I never had with my parents. But I find that I like being alone although I love him, and I'm glad to see him go when he visits.

Sometimes I feel so glad that I don't have my kids all the time. I spend the weekend with them and I'm exhausted by Sunday night.

I'm not the most patient person in the world, and I'm not sorry when they go home after a weekend, and I never feel lonely for them. I'm very happy when I'm with them, but I don't miss them when I'm not.

When my kids first went to live with their father I didn't want to sign over formal custody, but if he asked me to sign now I would because I don't want them to come back. I've changed my life-style. I have an apartment and a job I couldn't keep if they came back. I have all sorts of plans for myself. I'm exploring. I'm having a good time. I feel sometimes when I do see them that they're almost like an imposition—I have so many things I want to do with myself. I love them and I want to be with them, but when they do come I can't wait for them to leave. I'm still struggling financially. I don't have job satisfaction. I don't have a lover. But I am *better than I was, just inside myself, and I don't think I could be if I still had the children. I almost visualize them hanging around my neck.*

Changing Plans

In the course of our interviews we also encountered instances in which a child who had gone to live with the father later wished to return to the mother. Most women said they would be quick to take a child back if this situation arose or if they felt the child was not being well cared for.

My daughter has been living with her father for about ten years, but she's thirteen now and she's had a bad year. Lately they're not getting along as well as they used to. She seems to be getting sick a lot, and every few weeks I get a hysterical phone call from her. So now we're embarking on the next phase of this adventure, and she's coming back to me.

The situation seems to be very good right now, but I'm ongoingly concerned with the children, and I try to keep in touch with them every few days by phone. If I felt something were wrong or that they'd be better off with me, then I'd want to change the situation. And our agreement says if the children express a desire to live with me, then that will occur without conflict between me and my ex-husband. I just continue to monitor their development. I don't think this is the end of the story and we'll all live happily ever after. Any number of things could happen.

My children have always known from the very beginning of this arrangement that they could come to live with me any time they wanted. My daughter has always had keys to my apartment. It's open to her any time. She's too old now to want to move in with me, but my son might want to do that, and I'd welcome it if he did. Circumstances in my life have changed, and it would be much easier for me now to have a child living with me than it was several years ago when I was working and in school and my son was very young and needed constant care.

I could never have considered this if I hadn't known that my ex-husband would give our children a lot of love and care. He was an excellent parent, and that's what gave us the freedom to make this choice. But if I believed that that had changed in any way I would want them back with me, of course.

A few women we interviewed who had had a child request returning to them said that they were reluctant to take the child back. Some cited the child's welfare; others mentioned their own.

My son has been with my ex-husband for nearly a year now, and it's been a very stormy year. The problem is that I like this new arrangement. I like the freedom and the quiet with him gone. But he's unhappy and wants to come back home, and I'm not ready for him to come home, and I don't know how to make him feel good about that. I want him to feel that I love him and care for him, which I do, but I don't know how to deal with his phone calls and the sound of desperation. My therapist has counseled me that my son is probably not all that unhappy but just doesn't want to make the necessary adjustments to the new situation. He likes to be the center of attention, and he's not that with his father because there are two other children.

My second youngest daughter wants to come and live with me, but I've told her no. At this time I just don't think it's good for her. There's been enough upheaval over the last five years. I don't want her, or any of my kids, to think that relationships are that disposable: if you don't like what's going on you can just leave and come here or vice versa. I don't want to play a game of Ping-Pong with my children. At some point stability has to set in. Also, how do I explain to six children that I'm only going to take one? In their minds they'll think: you only love her, you don't love us. If I didn't think they were being adequately taken care of, they wouldn't be there.

The question the one mother raises—how to make her son feel good about her unwillingness to have him reside with her again—is an especially difficult and painful one. There probably is no way to make him feel "good" about that. But it is possible in such a situation to make clear to a child what the issues are and what they are not.

A participant in one of our workshops reported that her child said to her: "You say you love me but you won't take me back." And then the woman asked: "How can I answer that? What can I tell him?" The most positive response to that sort of question is: "I love you and I'm living alone now. I'm not saying I don't want you in my life. I'm not saying I don't want to be involved with you. I'm talking about living arrangements, not love." A negative response would include the phrase *I don't want you back,* a much too sweeping, all encompassing statement, and one that seems to imply total rejection, total abandonment.

An extremely important factor in the quality of part-time parenting is physical proximity to, or distance from, the children. Obviously a mother who lives near her children and sees them often is more likely, more able, to stay involved in her children's lives and to continue her parenting without the sharp break in continuity that distance creates. It is also obvious, or should be, that this benefits everyone: the mother, the father, and the children.

There is just no way to stress how crucial it is to be near your children. When I lived in the same city with them, it was wonderful. I could pick them up from school, meet them for a meal or a movie, have them come to my apartment whenever they wanted. We really saw a lot of each other, and even though we weren't literally under the same roof, I still felt I was very much their parent on a daily basis. But now they live an entire country away from me, and it's just impossible to keep up the same level of involvement. It doesn't have to do with my love for them or my interest in them diminishing. It just has to do with distance.

I've seen my kids at least every other weekend during the time they've been living with their father. But now I have a friend who lives just a few doors away from her ex-husband and the kids live there, and I see how they're in and out of her house all the time and it's really nice. It makes me wish in some ways that I had chosen to live even nearer to my kids.

The Short End of the Economic Stick

But while physical proximity may be the ideal, it is a fact of life in our society that people move around a great deal, perhaps most especially after a divorce. Often the visiting parent ends up living at some distance from his or her children. And this is another area in which women feel themselves at a disadvantage for economic reasons. A father who is a visiting parent is more likely to have funds available either to travel to his children or to have them travel to meet him. The financial scramble many women endured while they had custody of their children, the scramble that caused them to relinquish their kids in the first place, can continue to impede their relationships with their children when they have become visiting parents.

Now my sons are living several hundred miles away from me, and I don't see them very often because of economics. I'm working seven days a week, so I don't have time. When they lived with me, their father could always afford the time and money to have them visit him, but I just can't swing it very often.

At the moment I see my kids once a month, and even that is something of a strain because there's plane fare involved, and if I go there I have to rent a motel room where they can come to see me. My oldest son was telling me that he's angry I don't come to visit more often. I said I agreed I should come more but that I didn't have enough money to come twice a month. And that's the truth. I told him I have a new job and as soon as I begin to make more money I'll come to visit more often.

The Santa Claus Syndrome

The Santa Clause syndrome mentioned earlier is one that has special economic echoes for noncustodial mothers. There are some women, of course, who have financial resources as great as some men's and who are as likely to fall into the trap of lavishing material things on their children while stinting in the emotional area. But the majority of women are not in a position to do this. Even without the burden of supporting their children, they still come out on the short end of the economic stick.

Several of the women we interviewed mentioned how painful they found it to have to say no to their children when they requested a special treat during a visit. This pain was only exacerbated when the children made comparisons between their mother's saying no and their father's seemingly endless ability to provide them with whatever they wanted. Other women noted that, perhaps to compensate, they tended to be lenient with their children in nonmaterial ways. A few said they tended to bend over backward not to make visits "special" but rather to imbue them with a "normal" tone,

one that would exist between a mother and a child who lived together full-time.

I really get into avoiding conflict when I'm with my kids because we have limited time, and I want everything to be nice. Sometimes I'm too indulgent. I want the time to be good; I want the kids to know I love them. So I tend to let things go by that maybe I shouldn't.

My ex-husband indulges my son in toys, and I don't bring a lot of presents when I come to see him. I just bring me. It's also hard when I'm in the house not to be known as the one who plays. I'll do that sporadically, but I don't want them always to think, Mommy's coming. She'll play with me. They've finally gotten so that they let me do my own things while I'm there.

I've tended to be very lenient about visiting, very fearful about making demands on my kids. I was supposed to see them every third weekend, but it never came out to that because they'd have plans, things they wanted to do with their friends instead, and I wouldn't insist. But recently I have been letting them know my needs as a noncustodial parent. I've had to put my foot down and say, "I want to see you."

Sometimes I feel like I'm saying no to my kids just to balance out the way their father indulges them. But of course when I do that then I look like the bad guy, and I resent that.

I'm sure as a visiting parent that I treat my children differently in some ways than I would if I were living with them. There's a tendency, since time with them is limited, to avoid anything at all unpleasant. It seems so much worse to have a blow-up with a child when you don't live together. It gets blown out of proportion. Little flare-ups that you'd take completely in stride if you were living with them take on too much weight, too much significance. So you find yourself ducking anything that could possibly lead to a flare-up.

What There Is to Worry About—Later

One of the questions we asked in our interviews was: "What are your fears for the future?" Some of the fears the women named probably plague part-time fathers as well. Others are unique to part-time mothers.

My fear for the future is that I won't ever have my children with me and that my ex-husband will continue to work the children away from me.

My biggest fear is that my son won't work out things with his parents the way he should to become a true and free adult. He won't have a good healthy rebellion and work through it. If we have an argument, he can hop a bus and go home to Daddy. Things get short-circuited that way. I'm afraid he'll manipulate both me and his father into not confronting things. He'll play us off against each other, and then he'll suffer for it.

I don't know if brainwashing is too strong a word or not, but I'll use it. My ex-husband's thinking affects the children. He had a tremendous influence on their decision to live with him. He has a strong hold on them, and they do feel secure there. They feel safe. I think that's because no feelings get shown. It's a nice easygoing environment. I'm emotional and I used to show what I was feeling, and that made things more tumultuous, I suppose. But I'm afraid that the whole feeling side of them will die. I guess it's still up to me to keep that side of them alive in whatever ways I can. They know I'm available and that they can let their feelings out with me.

I think I was always much more involved in my children's emotional lives, and my husband was more involved in their active lives, which is probably true for most people of our generation. And I can continue to support my youngest son emotionally even though we no longer live together. But recently my husband's been seeing a lot of a woman he's interested in and he's rarely home, so I have this feeling, this fear, that my son is practically growing up alone. That's a matter of great concern for me.

When I was making the decision about what to do, the one person I did discuss it with was my oldest son, who was no longer living at home. "How much did you need me when you were fourteen (his brother's age)?" I asked him. "It wasn't that I needed you every minute," he said. "It was just that when I did need you I could just go to you, and you were there. Sometimes when I was going out, I'd look at myself in the mirror and think how ugly I was and how awful my clothes looked, and I'd feel how could I possibly go anywhere? Then I'd go and talk to you and you'd say I looked gorgeous, and I'd walk out feeling confident. Dad's never going to be able to do that." Well, I think of that a lot, and I still fear that my youngest son will wake up one morning and hate me—that fear is constant.

My relationship with my kids now is very good. As soon as we get together it's as though we haven't been separated. We have a closeness and an understanding between us. But I become fearful because my ex-husband seems increasingly to try to work them against me. So far they have withstood his efforts. But I worry about the future. I think ahead to graduations and weddings and worry will I be completely cut out of their lives? Will I never see them again? He seems truly determined to make things as hard on me as possible.

I guess my biggest fear is that no matter what I do or say that my children will carry with them a sense that I somehow rejected them. I handled the separation from them as well as I could have, I think. I reassured them over and over that it had nothing to do with my love for them. And they certainly seem to have accepted that. But on some very deep level I have this lingering fear that never goes away entirely, no matter how good things are between us.

For most women the role of visiting parent brings with it a mixture of positive and negative feelings, a jumble of fears and fantasies that are not easily categorized. There is no perfect solution to the dilemma of custody, and few of the women we interviewed were absolutely satisfied with their present living arrangements. On the other hand, none was completely dissatisfied.

I've had some very positive feelings about being without my children. The wonderful freedom, for one thing—picking up and going to a movie or a play or the ballet or going to see a friend, not having to chauffeur the kids around on their *schedule. I can read now. I have the time and quiet for it. I used to be too exhausted. I couldn't keep my eyes open. Eating when I want, sleeping when I want—I enjoy that.*

But I miss not having such a close relationship with people I brought into the world. And my guilt comes from having thought I left them in the care of someone whom I respected and who would give them the best. But now I fear I've left them with someone who will put a cloud of negativism over their heads because his anger with me is so great.

Even as I'm afraid and worried about what my working and being away from my daughters is doing to them, I'm also trying to share that time away with them. I'm trying to bring them into my work world in a very adult way in that I talk to them a lot about what I feel about what I'm doing. I want them to work with me, not in the kitchen, and I want them to see how I handle people, to see my managerial style. I'm conditioning them to know I really want to work with them. Fathers up and down Park Avenue bring their sons into the business. My fantasy is that I can do the same for my daughters. Where is it written that a woman can't bring her daughters in?

I belong to a Mothers Without Custody group, and we discuss the blessing and burdens of living apart from our children. I can sleep in any day I want—that's a blessing. Mother's Day—that's a burden. I'm always in a blue mood all of Mother's Day. Also the first day of school is bad for me. Buying clothes for my niece is hard too. These are strange things that you wouldn't predict. You don't always know when these feelings are going to hit.

I love taking a bath in private. I can go to the hairdresser without worrying about who's killing who. If I don't feel like cooking dinner, I don't have to. There are nice times. Plus, I like having thoughts of my own and being able to think for two hours without doing anything or being able to read the New York Times *from one end to the other on Sunday without having to worry about cooking breakfast or lunch. At home, the kids would get up early, and I'd make breakfast for them. The* Times *would arrive about ten o'clock. Then my husband would be up at eleven and want brunch, and I'd be cooking again, and by the time I cleaned up it was three in the afternoon and time to start thinking about dinner, and I never got to the* Times *until maybe Wednesday. I like being able to take care of myself.*

But it's bad when I have to take the kids back to the train after a visit. The sadness is awful. Or when I have to get on the train myself, going away from them, and have the littlest one kiss me good-bye and ask, "When am I going to see you again, Mommy?" Or, "Can't I stay longer, Mommy?" And when he's in the city and it's Sunday, he gets hard to handle because doesn't want to go back, and I have to deal with that properly or we'll both be in tears. It's happened. And it's very hard, although after it's over it sort of clears the air.

The loneliness is the hardest thing about all this. The best thing is being free to do anything I want when I want to do it and not having to own up to anybody.

SIX

Full-time Father

What about fathers who become primary caretakers? Certainly, they confront societal myths and assumptions just as mothers do. The sex-role stereotypes are just as strong for them: men are not nurturing or, if they are, they are not completely "masculine"; there is no such thing as a paternal instinct—women do naturally what men must learn to do and then, more than likely, do in an inferior fashion; men don't know how to run households and attend to all the tasks therein; and, of course, children do not belong with their fathers.

Some of the women we interviewed, however, reported that the father with whom they were leaving their children was the better parent, more nurturing, sometimes more stable than they. Many women said they felt that their children's fathers were certainly equal to them in their parenting abilities. The father's personality, parenting abilities, and desire to have his children live with him were important factors in these women's decisions. Our interviews with single fathers tended to bear out these assessments.

Most studies of single fathers distinguish between seekers, those fathers who actively wish to become single parents, and assenters, those fathers who accede to single fatherhood but don't seek it on their own. And most studies have found that the quality of the parental experience can differ widely between the two groups. We talked to fathers in both categories and found that even the nonseekers were quite capable of becoming committed parents over the long haul. Every one of the fathers we interviewed reported that he found the experience of raising his children alone a rich and rewarding one, despite its stresses and difficulties.

Hard Work—but Worth It

We had two children, a daughter and a son who were seven and four at the time of the divorce. First my wife had the children, but then I initiated the idea of the kids coming with me. At first she said no. Then several months later she changed her mind. I think she decided she couldn't cope well with both children. Also my daughter had been telling her that she wanted to live with me, and that influenced my wife to change her mind. I'd say my wife had a poor emotional relationship with the kids when we were living together and when they lived with her after we separated. She was inconsistent, anxious, frightened, and upset. So I got legal custody after the first year, and she paid some child support. We both wanted that arrangement.

When our daughter was born my wife went right back to work, and I was free in the afternoons so I was very involved with my daughter from the time of her birth. But once I had custody I was much more involved. I was doing what women have done for generations in terms of housework. I was also the director of counseling in a job corps center, which was a nine-to-five job. And the main problem I had was time—getting up and getting everyone together and to school and getting me to work and then later being available for homework and having a social life of my own. I pretty much limited my social life during the week though unless people wanted to come to my house.

I was never too uptight about being in the role of nurturer, but there was always a nagging sense of guilt about it: can I do this as well as a woman could? I was unable to present that magic quality of the maternal instinct. I thought a woman could naturally intuit a child's needs. I don't think that today.

Occasionally, people would say to me that I should get remarried so I'd have someone to help me with the kids. I knew that was the last thing I wanted to do, and because I haven't remarried I've invested a great deal of energy in my relationship with my children. That's very special to me.

It's hard work to take on your children. It's not easy; it's not romantic. But I'm fortunate that I've been able to manage the child-caring responsibilities of my children. I wouldn't change that for anything. I feel fortunate to have two children and to have been able to be a part of their lives. If we'd divorced and my wife had remarried and moved to the South, as she's since done, and taken the children with her, I would have looked on that as a real loss, a great tragedy in my life. I think men traditionally have lost out on a very important experience in life, and if there's any way for them to be involved with their children, through single parenthood or joint custody, they should take it.

No Loss of Role

When we decided to break up there was never any question of a custody battle. We both just assumed that we'd have joint custody. That was that. And I took the kids first because my wife was on leave of absence from the university and going away for a year and a half. The main horror to us was how we were going to break this to the kids who were seven and eight. So we sat them down and told them, and my daughter spoke first and said, "Well, I can understand what you two people are going to do, but what does this mean for us?" So we told them that they'd be living with me to begin with and then later on with Mom, and they said that was fine. We couldn't believe it. They seemed somehow to be of the impression that this was not a big catastrophe.

Now I don't believe that they just don't care. I don't know what it is, maybe they see so much of this, families breaking up, on television. Another thing was that they weren't losing a role from their lives. That was important, I'm sure. My wife always worked, and we always had child care, so this wasn't an enormous change. I can't say nothing happened. That would be stupid. But there were no major upheavals. They weren't brought up believing that Mommy is always there. In fact, in our house there was never a particular mother role or father role. Our kids never saw at home what the society thinks mommies do and daddies do. They saw two people playing essentially the same role, so I would suspect they can't say, "Hey, I lost a mother" or "Hey, I lost a father." There was no well-defined role that was suddenly dropping out of their life.

I must say at times it was very difficult for me as the single parent, although I had a housekeeper. I was dealing with all these people, but I was extremely lonely. And I had decided not to date and not to stay away from the house overnight for a one-year period. I didn't want any conflict. I didn't want the kids to feel my absence, and I made that my code, no matter how many invitations I got. And I kind of compensated for the loneliness by just being as busy as I could be. I just did things to occupy all of my time, and I'd fall asleep exhausted and wake up the next day and start all over again. But the bargain I made with myself was that I didn't want the kids to feel they were in the way. I didn't want them to feel that they came second to anything or that I was coming home just because I had to. I wanted them to know that I wanted to be with them.

A Great Head Start

I started raising my kids alone in 1959, and it was really almost unheard of then. Their mother was a jazz musician, and she wanted to be on the move, to be free to pursue her career. She was just having such a difficult time in the world workwise that I don't think she could bear the added responsibility of taking care of children. The kids were five and three then, and this situation wasn't something I particularly wanted, but it was something I readily accepted.

I didn't see having the kids as a great difficulty. And emotionally I had a lot of support. If you're a man with two children people give you credit for anything you do, and they excuse anything you don't do. It was really no burden. But any woman who lived with the children the way I did would have had the children taken away from her just for behaving the way I did, the way that was causing me to receive applause. I did things that would really give me pause today, but I got no disapproval for them.

Living by myself with the children, there were certain things that were like mountains to climb—like doing the laundry or knowing about clothes. I just had no organizational sense. If I got my own two socks the same color on a given day it was an accomplishment, so what did I know about working out outfits for my daughter that were attractive or pretty? We just had this big pile of clothes and she'd have to search through it for socks, underwear, a blouse. I just don't understand how parents coordinate their children's clothes; I just don't know how it's done.

Also in terms of food I wasn't very organized. I didn't prepare many meals although there was always plenty of food around. I kept the refrigerator filled. But it was a battle to keep our heads above water. Getting clothes clean and having meals were not things that were taken for granted. I see things differently now and I'd be a better parent now, but I don't have any regrets. And my kids are pretty healthy and basically sound.

I know this for sure. Whatever anyone says about a situation like this has to be taken with a grain of salt. I have my version of things, my kids would have another, their mother would have still another. Sometimes I'll glorify something I did at the time that I really needed as a defense for myself. I feel a sense of inadequacy about what I have provided, but maybe most parents feel that. And I think there's a continual need to justify, in whatever ways I can, what was. But I look at my kids now and I see how marvelous they are, and I feel so lucky.

You know, life is on our side raising kids. There is a spirit inside that wants to be, that's positive, that's healthy. If only parents could know they're not on trial, and everything isn't going to rise and fall on each action done or not done. This load of pressure and guilt and incapability is the biggest weight that single parents carry. If we could only know that there's something right to begin with that's on our side, it would relieve us of such a weight of guilt and anxiety and apprehension. Everything wouldn't be so fraught with significance. We wouldn't think that if we don't put braces on our kids' teeth or give them Tiger's Milk that their lives will be ruined. We're all given such a great head start. Everything doesn't just depend on what parents do and don't do.

Kids Are a Privilege

When our daughter was small and I was in school I spent a lot of time with her. I raised her really and I loved it. My wife really raised our son, and when she worked for her mother she took him along from the time he was very small. But by the time our kids were two and five things were very bad between my wife and me. We were going in different directions, becoming very different people.

My number-one concern was always what I could provide for my children, what I could give to them. At least I knew that we needed help. There were children involved, and when that's the case, then you don't screw up. You reach out and get help if that's what you need. Well, I went into therapy and the kids came too, but my wife wouldn't cooperate. Finally, she moved out of the house. I think she loves the kids, but she says the best thing she could have done was to leave them with me. She doesn't know how to handle them.

Other people seemed to look at me with pity or with praise. Oh, you poor guy. *I hate that. I wanted my kids.* Oh, you're wonderful. *I'm not so wonderful. I just did what had to be done. Then, of course, people also say, "I hope you find a new woman, a good mother for the kids." I never had a problem with washing diapers or cleaning floors or putting up curtains. Now I can't stand it because I had such a dose of it—but I was the stereotypical drudge, I did it all.*

But having those kids is a privilege. I believe that. I believe, dammit, you brought those kids into the world, so you pull yourself together and do what you have to do to provide for them. You're obligated to get them into a place where they can grow, have some peace, some joy, and learn. It's an awesome thing, a beautiful thing.

I wanted things for my children that I never had: freedom of expression, good parenting, loving but not too distant, not too close. You have to wear a hundred hats. Is it worth it? Yes. Would I do it again? Yes. Will I go on doing it? Yes. It's very hard. I don't know how women do it. But what job is there that's more important? Sure, I resented some things. But I gained much, much more. I gained a richness to my life, an understanding I never had before. I had to learn to be tender. Parts of me were called out by the experience of living alone with my kids that might never have surfaced otherwise.

Even Closer Now

We had one child together, and we were also raising two of my wife's children from another marriage. When we split up I said I wanted our daughter who was four and a half at the time. It only took my ex-wife a week or two to decide to leave the child with me. Economics may have played a part in her decision. But I was always more into being a parent than she was. She was into working and letting the kids shift for themselves.

Because I was working free-lance I was home to take care of my daughter until the time she went to school. We were always close, but we're even closer now that she lives exclusively with me. I don't see my role with her as full-time authority figure. I'm probably twenty percent authority, forty percent laissez-faire type, and forty percent pal. But now that it's just the two of us, I'm not distracted by other things. As soon as I had her to myself I gave her all my attention, and all her anger and frustration just disappeared. She became very calm. I was almost getting worried that there wasn't any reaction to the absence of her mother. All I saw was a positive reaction.

Making It Not a Job

I only saw my own father once in my entire life. I've never known how to be a father, and I always thought of myself as a bad father. But if something has to be done I'll do it. I don't cop out on anything. Taking care of the kids is like that. If their mother won't do it, I'll have to.

I always thought my wife was a great mother and a great wife with fantastic communication with all five of our kids. But a few years ago things started to change, and she started coming to work with me just to get out of the house and to get away from the kids. Then she started talking about leaving. She started seeing some other guy. And finally I said that she had to get out of the house. I said I had to be in charge of the house, and I couldn't do it with her sort of there and sort of not. All along she'd said that when she left she'd take the two youngest kids with her, but she didn't do that. Our daughter did eventually go to live with her mother though.

It's been a job having the kids, but I've tried to make it not a job, if you see what I mean. The most difficult things about it are finding enough time and making enough money. But time is the hardest thing. I still don't think I give the kids enough time. I have two days off a week, and one of them I still save for myself. I feel like I need the rest on that day. But I've been thinking about that and feeling I should spend part of that time with the kids also. I'm getting a lot closer to them now.

Not Willing to Trade

I was the main parent from the time our daughter was two or three. I enjoyed being a parent more than my wife did. She was capable of great love and warmth, but she was very inconsistent. Also, she didn't like the responsibility of being a mother.

She got involved with a spiritual group and wanted to live in this community for a period of time. She felt she'd get her head together with this guru and then come back. There was no doubt that our child would be with me. Eventually I realized that she wasn't coming back, and I started divorce proceedings. I had a lot of support through all this from a male friend, from my mother, and from my mother-in-law. My mother and mother-in-law were very angry at my wife, especially my mother-in-law. She didn't even want our daughter to visit her mother.

I wasn't angry about having my child with me. I wanted her. I still feel bad that she doesn't have a mother, but I enjoy being a parent. At times it's very pleasurable; at times it's very difficult. The hardest part of single parenting is going through it alone. There's no one to share it with. Some days it's hard for me to see my daughter's ups and downs. Some days it's a lot of fun. But whatever day it is, I wouldn't trade it. Raising her is an important part of my life. I think men can learn from their children. It's a rare opportunity for us to be more in touch with our own humanity.

Opening Up Emotionally

I agreed to take our kids because I thought it was fair for my wife to have a break and to be able to get herself established professionally.

She'd put me through school early in our marriage and, as she pointed out to me, she deserved her turn, and I agreed with that. But even though I was willing, I wasn't thrilled at the prospect of changing my life in the ways I knew I'd have to to accommodate the children. I had plenty of misgivings, believe me.

But now I feel grateful that my wife took the stand she did and that I was more or less forced into this. It's been an incredible experience for me. Not only have I gotten to know my children in whole new ways, I've also gotten to know so much more about myself. I think the whole experience has really opened me up emotionally. I've found that I possess certain qualities I never would have suspected in myself.

One thing I'm sure of is that the expectations for a single father are so much lower than they would be for a single mother and, as a result of that, I've had a lot of help and support. People will offer to do surprising things—things I'm perfectly capable of doing—because they assume that since I'm a man, I don't know how to do these things. Taking my daughter shopping for clothes, for example. Last fall I had no less than three offers of help with that even though it's something I can perfectly well do and actually enjoy doing. And at first, of course, I had neighbors offering me food all the time, the way they would have if someone had died, as if I weren't capable of cooking. I'm sure if I were a woman with her kids I wouldn't have had casseroles on my doorstep every evening.

It's not easy to take care of your kids alone. It's demanding and time-consuming, and it's sometimes quite lonely. But it's also a great pleasure. I have a wonderful time with my kids, and now I can't imagine my life without them. I would really have lost out on something important if I hadn't lived with them like this. And I wouldn't even have known I was missing it.

How Single Fatherhood Is Different

From the most reluctant to the most enthusiastic, all these men found positive aspects to the experience of single fatherhood. Some felt this very strongly, calling the experience a "privilege" and an "opportunity." It was clear that they would have felt cheated had they *not* ever served as their children's primary caretaker. Most of these men were involved, caring parents before their divorces. They had a stake in their children's lives that they were not willing to relinquish. The problems of having too little time and too much isolation were the main drawbacks cited by the single fathers we talked to, phenomena familiar to single mothers as well. Nowhere did we hear men complain about being unable to provide a nurturing, caring environment for their children, that aspect of parenting for which they are supposed to be so ill suited.

The differences between a father's experience of single parenthood and a mother's do not, in fact, turn up in those areas where they might be most expected. But there are differences, ones that come from the outside, from the society, rather than from inside the individuals themselves. These differences make single parenthood easier for some men than it is for some women. One difference is that men do not suffer the same economic pressures as single parents that women do. It is rare for a man to report that financial difficulties are a distinguishing feature of his single fatherhood.

One father we spoke with did mention not having enough money. But it was clear that he would have felt this were true had he and his children been in an intact family. The economic pressures had not increased since he had become a single parent. On the other hand, it was a commonplace for women to describe financial difficulties as an integral part of their single motherhood. Financial pressure, as we have noted, was one of the largest factors in causing women who have had custody of their children to relinquish it.

Another great difference between single motherhood and single fatherhood is that single fathers tend to get more help and support for their parenting efforts, while single mothers are supposed to make these same efforts, and more, with ease and aplomb and *without* assistance. When the single parent is the father, friends and families are quick to recognize what a difficult job it is, and supporters seem to appear magically to pitch in and help. When the single parent is the mother, the situation is treated as though it were part of the natural order of things, deserving of neither special help nor recognition. Taking care of children, after all, is what women are supposed to do and are able to do automatically. A single mother, however, may have just as great a struggle as a single father. Economically, she will be likely to have an even greater one. Yet her struggle will be virtually invisible to most people who encounter her and her children.

One single father we interviewed was a man who lived in the suburbs of a large city in the Midwest with his two children, a girl of nine and a boy of seven. His story encompassed most of the elements we encountered in our other interviews with fathers in this situation. And it seemed to us to embody the essence of what single fatherhood can be. For that reason we present his story in some detail. Listening to this thoughtful, conscientious, caring father truly gives the lie to easy assumptions that children living apart from their mothers have been "abandoned" and that men cannot be nurturing, sensitive parents.

Children Are Not Toys

I was married for twelve years, and I saw myself as very happily married, and I assumed it was for the rest of my life. I thought we'd buy dual tombstones. Then the next thing I knew my wife was fooling around, and she wanted to leave to be with her boyfriend who was her boss at that time. She made the obligatory noises about joint custody. I said no. She said okay. That was the extent of our custody battle. I don't mean to imply that she doesn't love the kids; she does. And I'm sure if you talked to her she'd swear she really wanted the children. But the fact was I would have done anything to keep my kids. I was losing her. I wasn't going to lose them too. Our relationships with other people define who we really are, and my kids were the most important thing in my life. It was wonderful just to be part of them. During our marriage we'd always split caring for the kids between us.

I guess stereotyping says I'm not supposed to want them so much. My brother said I should make her take the kids and then I could be a bachelor, free. I could get out there and have a good time. My lawyer said the same thing. He told me I was crazy to take them. Some of my friends also told me I was crazy. But my values said that I didn't bring those kids into the world as toys for me. They're not replaceable parts. They're human beings and they have needs, and I have a responsibility toward them.

My ex-wife is very bright, very attractive. She's a terrific person, and I'm sorry she left me. It wiped out my life for a couple of years. But the only negative place still left between us is about the time she spends with the kids. When we negotiated a separation agreement and started talking about visitation rights, I said I didn't want her to have visitation rights. I wanted her to have visitation responsibilities. Just because she doesn't love me anymore, that doesn't mean that she doesn't have responsibilities. She's still their mother. That's their right—they have a right to still have a mother. I wanted her to see them as much as she wanted to, and now my biggest hassle with her is to get her to see the kids more. It's like a real role reversal. She sees them now one night a week and every other weekend, but sometimes she negotiates away time and ends up seeing them only one weekend a month. The kids want more than that.

The first year and a half that I had the kids I tried to be all things to everybody. We went through a time we'd all like never to go through again. I wanted to prove I could be a good mother too. Frankly, what I got from that was peptic ulcer disease. The fact is that if you're going to make the commitment to be a parent, you have to be willing to be frustrated, to not always be perfect. More and more now I try to let my kids know that I have limits—I'm not God. I know how to iron but I cannot sew worth a goddamn, and I try to let them see that. They can make demands on their mother for some of the things I can't give them. Now I allow a little more vulnerability to show to the kids. I allow them to be part of my life in that way.

At first I thought if I hired a housekeeper that meant I was a failure. But that's the best money I ever spent. At first, when I got into showing what a great homemaker I was, I'd make all these fantastic meals, and my kids would look at them and go yuck. *And that hurt like hell. I've always been a good cook, but I learned to cook more simply for them. One of our rules now is that you don't have to eat what I make for dinner, but you do have to have a meal, so cook it yourself. Then we rotate the cleaning up. That rule has changed our lives.*

I've learned that I wouldn't trade my kids for anything, but I wouldn't want another. The practical concerns are enormous. It's a very heavy number to do everything alone. I'm one hundred percent responsible for them, and that responsibility is awesome. And people in my situation don't get any help from the society, you know. Our society hates the situation of the single parent. For example, in the first year after the divorce my son was having some reading problems. So I went to his teacher and she said, "Well, his problems are caused by the broken home." I said, "What have you been reading, some 1930's novel?" That infuriated me! I said, "Face the fact that half your kids are in this same situation and get rid of your antique attitudes. Also, a broken home and his reading problem may not go together. He may just have a reading problem. And what if you're right? Let's suppose you are. What should I do? Get married again? I can't get remarried just to improve my kid's reading." And finally I said, "What are you going to do about his reading problem? And what do you want me to do? I'll support you however I can." That broken home stuff is useless. It's just psychological gossip, a judgment. It doesn't help anything. And it usually doesn't end up leading to any plan to change anything.

Another thing that's garbage is this insidious thing about quality time versus quantity time. I've learned that that's such a lie. You can't always have quality time when you want it, by decree. Your kid may not be ready for the wonderful quality hour you want to give. He may have something else in mind. The whole concept of quality versus quantity is a nice sop to people like me who have busy schedules and a lot of guilt feelings.

I've experienced a lot of sexism in this situation. Solicitors call up and ask for the woman of the house, and when I say there isn't one, they hang up. Trying to get a housekeeper for the evenings when I was teaching was really hard. I'd say I was a divorced man, and they'd hang up on me. One woman actually said to me, "I don't want to work for a divorced man." The family next door to us feels the wrong parent got the children, and she sometimes comes over to give the kids some nurturing she's sure they're missing. So whenever I bake something I send some over to her, which is by way of saying,

"Look, I can do it too. You don't have to have breasts to operate an oven."

Most fathers think fathering consists of a few surface tasks, tossing the kids up and down a few times on the front lawn and then retiring behind the newspaper. But fathers can learn how to father if they want to. One of the most insulting things is when people say to me, "Oh, you're mommy and *daddy." And I say, "No, I'm just daddy, and that's enough." Daddy can be very nurturing. People assume that kids in this situation are missing half of what they should have. Well, my kids might miss their mother as a person, but as far as having a nurturing parent, they're getting that.*

By the way, I'd say don't become a single parent if you can possibly avoid it. Stay married, if you can, if you can find a way to be happy. Try to work it out. Forgive the other person if they've messed up one time. Being a single parent is probably the loneliest job in the whole world. Any help you're going to get ends at ten at night when the housekeeper goes home and it's too late to call people to talk. That's when you discover what it's really like to be a single parent. All the rest of the time you're moving around doing tasks. The other part of it, of course, is that it's joyful, delightful. The possibilities are intense.

No one can survive without support so it's important to educate your support system. I've had to let my friends know what kind of advice I need, what kind I don't. I had to let people know my needs. I'd ask them to call every week or so, just so I'd know someone was thinking of me.

The whole issue of masculinity has never come up for me. And anyone who would think that way—well, I wouldn't be interested in what they'd think. That's their problem. The funny thing about this situation is that it seems to have made me more attractive to women. It's certainly not especially romantic in my home though. And if you want to get into any sexual activity, there are always monitors. But it really snows any woman who's ever seen the relationship I have with my kids.

You know, this isn't anything you should take on if you think you're just going to try it out and then in a year toss it back to your ex-wife. Kids aren't Ping-Pong balls. That will feel like double rejection to them. You shouldn't take this on if you don't take some delight in the prospect. I guess that was the main thing I had in my favor: a real desire to be with my children. I was *an abandoned child. My father ran off with another lady and left my brother, my mother, and me, and I never heard from him again. When my mother remarried I was hysterically happy to have a father again. But while I was growing up, my mother constantly told us how much she was sacrificing for us.*

My kids, on the other hand, get the message that I'm delighted to be with them, that they're a treat for me to have, and they really are. I get more from them than they could ever get from me. They give me a sense of immortality, constant love. They're kids but they're also really lovely people to know. And I have to ask, after all, what am I living for?

SEVEN

Court

When we told our kids we were separating, they said, "Why aren't you and Daddy going to court to fight over us like they do on television?"

This question could only be asked by an innocent. Custody battles are debilitating, destructive experiences for all the parties involved, and most caring, well-meaning parents try to avoid court. Nearly any alternative way of reaching a custody determination is preferable. As a matrimonial law expert with whom we spoke put it, "If it gets to court, everyone loses."

Whenever I have clients considering a custody battle, I sit them down and show them a file filled with about fifteen inches of paper. I tell them that they'll be at the mercy of court-appointed psychiatrists, social workers, physicians, schoolteachers. Employers might possibly be dragged in. I explain every aspect of what their potential exposure is. And then I highlight—and every serious, caring attorney would—the emotional trauma involved, trauma shared by attorney and client alike.

Despite the well-publicized horrors of custody battles, an estimated ten to fifteen percent of custody decisions are made in court. Our purpose in this book has not been to scrutinize instances in which mothers have lost their children through the courts. Rather, we have focused on women who have *chosen* to live apart from their children. Yet we have seen that in many cases court, or the mere idea of it, has frequently been a factor in that choice. Often, if a mother is on the fence about custody, the simple threat of going to court will quickly topple her, and she will come down on the side of acquiescence to her husband's wishes.

To Avoid the Worst

I had thought I would take the kids with me when my husband and I separated. Two of them were still quite young, and I just thought it would be best if I had them, even though I knew it would be hard for me financially and maybe in some other ways too. I wanted to go back to school, and it would have been hard to work that around the kids' schedules. I would have needed some extra help, which I probably couldn't afford.

But then my husband said he'd like the kids. Well, I thought about that, I considered it; but I still thought I'd prefer having them with me. Then he said he'd go to court if he had to, that he really wanted them that much. When I heard that, I just buckled. The whole idea of going to court was horrendous to me. But I knew he was serious; he meant it. I would have agreed to practically anything to avoid going to court.

As it turned out, it was fine that the kids stayed with him. I did go back to school, and that's been easier to manage without the kids. He's a good father. He really cares about his kids, and he's become a much more involved parent since he's had them living alone with him. The kids seem fine. So it's really been all right. And now I can see maybe this way has even been the best way for us all. But I wouldn't have done it if he hadn't threatened me with court, and there's something about that that has always galled me a little.

The Irony of Bias

Nowhere in our interviews did we encounter a woman who was *not* fearful of court. Some women describe their fear in quite vivid terms. They are afraid that in court they will "go to pieces," "fall apart," "collapse." They seem to imagine being utterly victimized. Other women characterize their anxieties about court as a sort of general apprehension.

First, we should note the irony inherent in this. Custody cases are in fact one of those rare areas where, traditionally, a bias has existed in favor of women. The maternal-preference rule gave this bias legal form: the child was presumed to be better off with its natural mother. Even though that presumption has now been wiped out legally and the guideline for determining custody is "the best interests of the child" doctrine, the bias in favor of the natural mother still exists. Custody decisions, after all, are rendered by judges. And judges are just human beings who bring to their decision-making their own philosophies and prejudices—conscious and unconscious—their own ideas, and the models with which they have grown up. Those things cannot be eradicated by changing a law on the books. So philosophically, as well as statistically, the custody deck is still stacked in favor of the natural mother. Even so, mothers experience tremendous fear at even the contemplation of a custody battle.

I realized that if I was going to push to keep the children we would have had to go to court. That loomed as an absolute horror for me. I felt very incompetent in this area. My sense was that this was my husband's realm and that I'd just be crushed. Everything to do with the whole legal end of things was very difficult for me. I found even the idea of choosing an attorney intimidating. And thinking about the money that a lawyer would cost was frightening.

My husband's pressuring me to give him custody. I don't know what I want. I don't know whether I could go through a court battle or not. It scares me. I've spent my whole life acquiescing, running from conflict. The idea of having to fight is horrible to me. But this involves my children, and I have to make a decision. Will I go to court or not?

I felt like I'd never won an argument with my husband in our entire life together. So the idea of arguing on a grand scale—in court, with lawyers and judges and witnesses and experts—was com-

pletely terrifying to me. It was just so obviously unacceptable that I agreed my husband could have the kids from the first time he even raised the idea of court. Now I look back on that and wonder if he would have carried through. Maybe, maybe not. The point is that I couldn't even consider it clearly because of my fear. I suppose he knew that. It was smart.

The Unhappy Past, the Idea of Harm

What makes the notion of court carry such weight? Why is it so potent? For one thing, though the laws on the books today have changed, women still have extremely unpleasant associations with custody suits. In the past, for a husband to gain custody of his children, it was mandatory that he attempt to demolish his wife in court. That was necessary if he was to prove her unfit and thus gain his children by default. And nothing short of utter destruction would do the trick. That was how strong the maternal preference rule was. Though the same standards no longer apply, the old associations are not so easy to shrug off.

Aside from the likelihood of character annihilation, another thing women conjure up when they contemplate a custody case is the idea of harm to the children. All of us probably carry in our imaginations some emblematic custody horror story that we picked up from the movies, a book, or newspaper accounts of an actual case: a child is hauled before a courtroom filled with people and asked to choose which parent he or she wants to live with, a child on the witness stand testifying for one parent, against the other, a wailing child being wrested from the arms of one parent and handed to another beneath the eyes of the judge. Whatever the specific content of our image, the general notion of damage done and havoc wreaked comes through, as well it should. Custody cases *are* destructive to children, and women's awareness of this is certainly a factor underlying their fear of court. No conscientious mother wants to expose her children to the injury a custody case can inflict.

Issues That Have Nothing to Do with the Issue

A wish to protect their children and an uneasiness created by old associations are not the only reasons the prospect of court seems to trigger such apprehension in so many women. Whether they choose to acknowledge it or not, opposing parties in a custody suit are quite often, perhaps most often, fighting over issues that have nothing at all to do with the best interests of the child. This is unfortunate but, alas, extremely common. The children in fact may be the last thing on anyone's mind in a custody case even though they are, ostensibly, the prize being fought over. A desire to inflict revenge on a spouse, a need to defeat a spouse by "winning" in court, a hope of healing a bruised ego by being proclaimed the victor in a legal skirmish—all these are much more common motives for custody battles than is the honest attempt to determine what will best insure a child's welfare and happiness. In other words, custody cases tend to be about power and the effort to exercise it, symbolically or otherwise. And when power is the issue between men and women, women will tend to feel at a disadvantage.

> *In my practice as a matrimonial lawyer I have found that all too often men bring in utterly frivolous claims. Let's say they've seen* Kramer vs. Kramer *and a few TV shows about custody, and suddenly they believe they're the better parent. But this is based on nothing really. The father in some instances neither wants the child nor is the better parent. He's simply acting out of pride, ego, revenge, bitterness. He's acting out of the need to say, "Look, you don't have the final say." Of course there are also fathers with legitimate claims, but the men making frivolous claims are hurting them.*

Consciously or unconsciously, women realize what is really going on in many custody cases, and their fear becomes understandable if we see it in that light. Their sense is that a court case is an effort to punish, even obliterate, them in a legitimate public forum rather than an expression of desire for the children. And at the very heart of that effort is a desire to strip them of what may be their two most valuable assets: their children and their self-esteem. Consciously or not, women know very well that when they enter court they are not about to participate in a dispassionate, impartial inquiry into the relative merits of each parent's parenting abilities. They know they are going into battle, and historically women are not used to winning power struggles with men. It is only recently in fact that women in large numbers have begun to recognize that they must learn how to fight. So it is understandable that women greet the possibility of court with trepidation and alarm.

Being "Judged" a Bad Parent

I raised my kids from birth to the ages of ten and thirteen, a son and a daughter. Then they went to live with their father just six blocks away. I was on welfare and we made this arrangement to give me a break, but I still saw them often and I still had custody. Well, I felt very good with all this time to myself, and I got a job and was doing very well. And then something happened and my daughter refused to see me. I didn't know why but for six months I saw only my son. So I went to a lawyer, and since I had custody he advised me just to go to their father's house and take them back with me, which I did. Their father then immediately took me to court.

I was very frightened by all this, but people said to me, "Don't worry. Nobody loses custody unless they're a junkie. It'll be fine. You have nothing to worry about. All you have to do is show up." So I began to believe that, and I wasn't even really prepared to defend myself. Well, the minute the proceedings started I was slapped in the face with a brief affair I'd had with my husband's brother after my husband and I had separated.

This judge I had was the worst possible one for me, I guess. He was a ninety-year-old Italian, and he just grabbed hold of this one issue and everything turned on that. He attacked anyone who defended me, all my witnesses. He'd scream at them, "Do you think a woman who'd have an affair with her husband's brother while she was living with her children is a fit mother?" The issue of who was the better parent was never even raised in court. And the kids' father was awarded custody.

That was a year and a half ago, and I haven't been the same since.

I feel like someone with a scarlet letter on my chest. My main problem is how this has left me feeling about myself. I feel that judgment that the court made. I see my kids now during the week and every other weekend, but I can't get over this bad mother *feeling. I think my daughter thinks that we went into that courtroom and I was judged a bad parent. Now I think she feels part of her is bad because she's a part of me. But I can't tell her what really went on without saying what a louse her father is. I can't tell her we never even discussed the issue of who was the better parent.*

This story embodies the fears and fantasies that so many women have about court: the feelings of impotence and intimidation; the inability to get one's case across; the humiliation of public censure; the damaged self-esteem; the harmful results for the children. Who wouldn't want to avoid such pain and distress? Yet there is a catch. Just as some women may be judged harshly for putting their children through a court battle, others may feel that they have to go through a court procedure to keep negative judgments at bay, both their own and the judgments of others.

I knew that I didn't want to be a wife or a mother at that point in my life, so I'd left my son with my husband. Then everyone in my family began telling me that I had to fight for my son. I was falling apart, desperate, scared, unemployed. We had a terrible court battle, and I was doing this because it was something I was supposed to do. People were telling me I should. But in fact I really wasn't ready to have my son with me. I was so confused. We ended up with joint custody, but the court battle really solved nothing. It just ate up a lot of money I could have used for school. It only made things much, much worse. I think my ex-husband set out to destroy me because I had the nerve to leave him.

"You have to fight for those kids. You can't just let him have them. They'll never survive with him. It's up to you to fight." That was the sort of stuff my mother kept telling me, and finally I gave in to that pressure and started legal prodeedings. She was thrilled and I was miserable, and finally I saw what I was doing and just stopped in my tracks and said he could have the kids live with him and we'd

have joint custody. That was really what we both wanted but of course my mother couldn't believe that. She could only see the whole thing as some awful plot of my ex-husband's against me and her grandchildren.

It wasn't that at all of course, but it was very hard to resist the sort of pressure she was putting on me. She made me feel as though I was some kind of uncaring monster if I didn't "fight." It's such a confusing time, and sometimes you listen to the voices that are loudest, even though they may not be the sanest. I wasn't all that clear then on what was the best course for each of us. So when somebody started pushing me, I went along.

Fighting for the Children

Going to court may sometimes be another one of those ways that women hide from themselves the true nature of their needs and desires. To "lose" one's children in court may seem a more legitimate way to separate from them than to recognize that living apart from one's children is an admissible preference. A woman can point to the fact that she "fought" for her children. She can argue that surely she wouldn't have fought if she hadn't wanted them. So it is on the record that this is a mother who wanted her children. That makes her a "natural" mother. There is nothing for which she need reproach herself.

As noted in Chapter 3, however, this process, which is in the main unconscious, seems to have long-range effects that leave these women in a much more precarious condition than those who have honestly examined their own motives and made a decision based on those motives to live apart from their children. Women who go through the motions of a custody battle and manage to separate from their children that way, rather than acknowledging that life apart from daily caretaking of their children is something they truly desire, pay a heavy price. Having adopted the stance of victimhood, they are often hard pressed to let go of it. Their ability to find anything strong and positive in their lives without their children is meager. They seem to cling to their anger and pain. A sense of hopelessness, a feeling of a lack of control over events pervades their lives. Frequently they are depressed and remain so for long periods. Unable to take the responsibility for their own desires, they now feel unable to take the responsibility for their own lives. By attempting to achieve something by a circuitous, rather than a direct, route, they have been left with a legacy of powerlessness. They chose to have something taken from them rather than to let go of it themselves. What began as a tactical stance has now become a reality.

By contrast, as we also noted in the third chapter, those women who were able to recognize what they wanted and needed and to state it clearly were distinguished by a sense of control over their own lives and feelings of positiveness and strength. It was clear that these women felt much more in charge of themselves and possessed of the power to make of their lives what they wished.

Some women may stop short of going through with a court battle and report that they are letting their children stay with the father just to avoid a nasty custody case. And sometimes this may be an honest account of a woman's motivation. But there are other instances in which this too may be another way for a mother to obscure her true needs and wants from herself and from others.

It is not difficult to understand why some women fall into this pattern of concealment. We have seen how culturally unacceptable it is for a mother to live apart from her children, and many women are not willing to place themselves so at odds with society's standards. The route of obfuscation, of shaded motives, of half-truths may seem more palatable. But women who choose this method of operation often suffer some of the same penalties as the women we mentioned above. Not having taken full responsibility for their feelings in the decision to live apart from their children, they too may suffer a residual sense of powerlessness, lack of control, and lack of strength.

Again, it is those women who are able to acknowledge directly what it is they need and want who appear to come through this most difficult and painful process in the most positive way. And this attitude seems also to bode well for their future as part-time parents. They have experienced an affirmation, rather than a negation, of self. That is likely to make them more able to give to and care for their children than someone who is feeling that she has lost something or had something taken from her.

Intimidation for a Lesbian Mother

One group of women for whom court is particularly frightening is lesbian mothers. The threat of a court battle is an especially heavy club over their heads. This is so for two reasons. Some women may not wish to have their lesbianism revealed publicly. They will stay out of court just to avoid that. Others may not care about the disclosure of their sexual preferences, but, at the same time they recognize that their lesbianism can be a potent weapon against them in court. While in recent years there have been some cases of lesbian mothers being awarded custody, the preponderance of court decisions have not been in their favor.

One lesbian mother who felt the climate of our society had changed in this regard discovered in a most disturbing fashion that it had not, at least not for her.

I'd been married ten years and had an eleven-year-old daughter when I went into a real sexual-identity crisis. I couldn't deny that I had sexual feelings for women. My husband told me that it was a crazy fantasy, and I went into therapy to try to "get over it." When I'd been in therapy a short time I realized that I had to get out of my marriage. It really was a farce. One night my husband hit me, and I left the house. I went back the next day, but he had locked me out. He wouldn't let me see my daughter.

So I went to a lawyer, a woman lawyer, and we decided to go to court. She said I'd have to decide if I wanted to bring out the gay issue in court or not. I finally decided that I would. It wasn't something I was ashamed of. I had begun a lesbian relationship a few months after leaving my husband. I felt quite secure about this in terms of my daughter. I felt I had raised her in an unslanted fashion and that I would be able to show this. I felt I'd been a very good mother.

Well, the first time we went to court the judge ordered that I see her only on Sundays from noon to six at her father's house. I wasn't to take her away from there until there were psychiatric tests done on all of us. My diagnosis came back Homosexuality with a capital H. There was no diagnosis for my husband. And my daughter was given the old "adjustment reaction to childhood" diagnosis. So the same restrictions on my seeing my daughter remained in place while we waited to go to court. In the meantime, the relationship I was in broke up because of the threat of my lover testifying in court about our relationship. She had a career to think of, and the whole thing made her very nervous. Also, my daughter was overwhelmed by everything that was happening.

We went through several court appearances and finally all the way to the municipality's supreme court, where a woman judge denied me custody. Despite all the testimony that I was and am an ideal mother, I think she was just appalled by my sexuality, and she gave the child to my ex-husband. That was a real double whammy for me. I work for a child protection agency and I see all these abused children, and very often I'm in the position of sending these kids who have been abused back into their families. All I can think then is: and I can't even have my own child.

Hearing stories like this, it is no wonder that lesbian mothers can be intimidated by the threat of court.

Anytime anything has come up to do with the custody of the kids there is always the implicit threat of court, of exposing me as a lesbian, hovering in the background. My ex-husband has never even said it directly. But he doesn't need to. Just the idea that it's there keeps me from taking a stand, and I think he knows that.

The first time it came up was when the kids went to live with him. There were a lot of things in favor of that, but what really clinched it was that I knew he would fight me if I didn't give in. Then there came a time when he was going to move some distance away, and I didn't want him to, but I didn't really put my foot down because I knew he'd be prepared to go to court if he had to. Now my daughter is about to go off to college, but I'd really like to have my son come live with me. If he wanted to come with me, I'd like to have him. And now I think I'd be prepared to go to court if I had to. But I'm not sure of that. It's still a very alarming prospect.

I'm an "out" lesbian so it doesn't bother me to think of having that revealed. But it does bother me to have it treated as something awful that might disqualify me as a mother. There are other reasons I know I wouldn't want to go to court—it's an awful thing for a child to witness, I think—but having my sexuality treated as an illness, as a perversion, is the biggest reason of all.

I generally feel good about myself. I'm not ashamed of being a lesbian. But I don't think I'd walk into a situation where I knew that that would be turned against me.

The other side of this coin is the account we heard of a lesbian mother and her ex-husband who worked out an arrangement between them regarding their children that they felt best served everyone involved. They were reluctant, however, to take it to court to make it binding because they feared that the court might upset what they had worked out as the best possible arrangement for them.

Is Court the Best Place to Decide?

What we hear in this and in many of the other fears and hesitations about court is a question frequently raised about custody matters: do they belong in court at all? Is a court the best place to decide such things? This question has been debated vigorously in recent years as divorces have increased and funneled a correspondingly heavy load of family matters into the court system. Even attorneys like the one speaking below, are able to see its shortcomings at the same time as they defend it.

The court system is sometimes completely and totally inadequate to handle the sort of things it's asked to handle. And it's sometimes at its most inadequate in the area of matrimonial law. It's like a machine that chews everyone up and spits them out in little pieces.

The decisions judges are asked to make are a very, very heavy burden. But, having said that, I haven't to date read or heard about any alternative that would work as well.

I'm against taking the attorney out of the process altogether because people need to be educated as to what their rights are before they can agree to give them up or agree to take something that they believe is their right. For example, how about a wife who's dealing with a divorce and is at her emotionally lowest level? She's ready to give up everything because unconsciously she feels she's not worth anything. Divorce strikes people's hearts, minds and emotions in completely unpredictable ways.

Or let's say there's a couple and the man knows his wife can get half of everything he owns so he decides to give her half of everything. He gives her half of the house, where she stays, half of his salary, half of any other property, etcetera. Meanwhile, he's not living in the house. He's taken on the additional cost of his own apartment. Because of his guilt and his lack of knowledge, he's given up something that not only hurts him but that his wife couldn't have obtained in the best decision in the world.

It should at least be explained what the parties are giving up and taking away. And then sometimes, of course, a fight is necessary, if one party is being completely unreasonable.

Mediation—Assessing the True Goals

Many different proposals have been made for alternative ways of dealing with divorce and related matters, the most important of which is custody. And one of these alternatives, divorce mediation, does remove the attorney from the process in any but an advisory capacity. Divorce mediation allows a husband and wife to negotiate their own divorce in an equitable manner and in a benign, non-adversarial environment with the help of a trained professional. Attorneys may serve as consultants to the divorce mediation process, but they offer guidance only, not legal advice.

Divorce mediation is certainly not for every couple. As the director of one divorce mediation program put it: "If your desire, conscious or unconscious, is to mutilate the other person, then you don't want mediation. But if there's a certain amount of goodwill, then you might want it."

A divorce mediation program we observed on Long Island was the first of its kind in the region when it began in 1977. Originally, its intent was to effect reconciliations between people considering divorce. It was believed that if couples could keep the lines of communication open, through the help of a trained mediator, they might come to abandon the idea of divorce altogether. In fact, few reconciliations occurred. But the director of the program stuck with the idea of mediation during divorce in the hope that all members of the family might benefit from it. The evidence would seem to indicate that they have, perhaps most especially the children.

Briefly, the way divorce mediation works is this: The divorcing couple comes together with a mediator, generally a mental-health practitioner who has been trained specifically for divorce mediation work. Together they work through all the issues that must be settled, trying to keep the grounds for the divorce, the idea of fault, out of the mediation process, concentrating instead on drawing up the best possible agreement. When they have done so, when all the issues have been resolved, the couple then takes the agreement to their respective attorneys, or to a single attorney, to have it translated into legal form and to be properly filed.

This sort of civilized, rational approach to divorce would seem to have obvious benefits for a divorcing couple. But it may be their children who gain the most. Mediation forces the involved parties to focus on the best interests of the children and to move away from using them as pawns in their struggle with each other.

> *In divorce mediation the myth of the child-oriented culture is truly exposed. The parents may use the phrase "the best interests of the children," but they're really focused on narcissistic needs of their own. We don't trust protestations of interest in the children. We try to cut through that and show them that they're not really interested in their children or they wouldn't be behaving the way they are.*

A mediator is trained to assess the *true* goals of each party. For instance, a mother may come into the mediation process insisting that the children live with her when in fact she is simply reflecting what society has conditioned her to believe that she wants. The mother may not even be aware of this. But a mediator will be able to help her discover that what she would really prefer is to live apart from her children, that that is what she is best suited for, that her personality and/or her current needs indicate that she might prefer the role of visiting, rather than custodial, parent.

Or take another example: a father who is determined to have his children with him, who offers protestations of undying interest in his kids, who contends he would be the better full-time parent. A mediator may discover that this man's children are the last thing on his conscience—that actually, he wants to inflict the maximum hurt on his wife, and trying to wrest her children from her is the way he can best imagine doing this.

We have already noted the benefits that can be gleaned from being open and honest about one's motivations in the midst of the divorce process. Parents who can realistically, candidly assess their parental abilities and desires are probably going to end up being better parents than those who labor under the necessity of trying to be something they are not. Mediation certainly is an aid to achieving that candor.

Mediation is also helpful to the children in what it demonstrates to them about their parents. Just the fact that a mother and father are willing to engage in this process tells the children that their parents are still parents, capable adults who can continue to take care of them. Imagine the difference between children witnessing this sort of behavior and children who are forced to watch their parents acting out their destructive emotions.

Mediators also stress how damaging it is for one parent to vilify the other in front of their children. Because children are so closely identified with their parents, an attack on either the mother or the father can feel as though it is being directed at the child. Urging parents to abjure this is another way the divorce mediation process protects children.

Conflict between parents is lessened in the process of divorce mediation whereas in the adversarial system it is exacerbated by the parties going to separate attorneys, each of whom is trained to look out for the best interests of his client, whatever the consequences for the other party and for the children. Any time conflict between parents diminishes, the children benefit.

Divorce mediators also cite another long-range advantage of the mediation process. When couples make up their own agreements, mediators contend, they are more likely to abide by them. Agreements that emerge from the adversarial system often fall by the wayside after a few years or, at the very least, continue to engender conflict. Agreements that people have fashioned themselves, agreements they believe are the best possible contracts they could have arrived at, tend to be more binding over the long haul.

Attorney vs. Mediator

Just as attorneys will argue that their services are crucial to the process of divorce, so mediators will insist that their skills are necessary to effect viable and humane divorce agreements.

> *We see a lot of anxiety and depression and guilt and shame. Attorneys are ill-equipped to deal with emotions that are simply part of every divorce.*

Attorneys, of course, readily rebut this.

> *Many divorce mediators only address the emotional issues. All they want to do is to keep the parties from fighting. They may tend to sacrifice a practical, solid settlement out of regard for the emotions. Sometimes a fight is a good catharsis too.*
>
> *Also, every good lawyer will try to see what the real issues are and to get the combatants away from the emotional arena into the practical arena. I often suggest counseling to help couples clarify*

issues. And whenever I see a parent who is basing custody ideas on emotion rather than on the best interests of the child, I always suggest getting some professional help with it.

A matrimonial lawyer is 90 percent psychology and 10 percent law. That's part of the joy and part of the heartache as far as I'm concerned. You're in the midst of great emotional trauma, and my job is to shield my client from that as much as possible and to be there when they need me. Good matrimonial lawyers are those who can successfully direct their clients in a healthy way.

Certainly there are competent, caring attorneys who can be sensitive to the emotional nuances of a divorce situation. But for every such lawyer there is another one who seems to make things more, rather than less, difficult.

The first thing my lawyer said to me was, "So you abandoned your children." I couldn't believe my ears. What that remark said to me was that I would have to fight my lawyer as well as my husband. That seems pretty overwhelming.

I think I did the right thing at the time to stay out of court and let my son go to his father. I really was just too damn sick to take care of him. But I would have preferred to have joint custody. My lawyer didn't want to go for that because it was a pain in the ass for him. It would have involved a longer, more drawn-out agreement. Things would have to have been spelled out more carefully. But as it is now I feel as if my son's life is completely out of my hands.

I'm having a bad time right now because my lawyer just told me that he wants $16,000 for a custody case, with $8,000 up front by next week. That's a lot of pressure. That means hocking jewelry and I don't know what else. He keeps urging me to go to my parents, and I said I will not. I've decided I'd like to have my two youngest kids with me, and my lawyer tells me that the biggest battle will be because I left the house. The worst part of this is that I thought joint custody meant that the kids live six months with one parent, six months with the other. That's what I expected. And nobody told me otherwise.

Divorce mediators are quick to say that they have a bias in favor of joint custody, even while acknowledging that it is not possible in every case. This bias is based on a conviction that a child needs to have the fullest possible access to both parents. Even if the joint custody involves no substantial time-sharing, even if it is in the main a symbolic designation, mediators say that the psychological tie is important. It binds both parents to the child and increases the child's chances of continued parenting, continued involvement, by both parties.

An attorney, of course, may argue that he has the same goal.

> *Any good attorney ought to be able to end up with an arrangement where both parents can share in the child-rearing decisions. No parent should ever feel after a divorce that they have lost their fatherhood or motherhood badge in the course of that divorce. No parent should ever feel that they have lost their stake in their child. This arrangement may not even be called joint custody. It can be stipulated though that both parents share in the decisions and that both must have the right to consent in major decisions. I'm more interested in results than in what the arrangement is called. It's the concept of joint custody that I'm interested in. Joint custody is really a plan for joint nurturing with both parents having equal input.*

Divorce mediation is not, of course, the only alternative that has been suggested to our present legal method of determining custody. Some of the suggestions center on reform of the present legal system; others are extrajudicial, taking the matter of custody out of the courts altogether and, for example, placing it in the hands of an agency staffed by child-care experts. One common feature of every one of these alternatives is some sort of impartial arbitration.

Our purpose is not to endorse any one of these alternative procedures for determining custody but rather to subscribe to that one common feature. Moving away from the adversarial system with its emphasis on conflict, a system where the whole point is to "win," and where the children all too easily get demolished in the skirmishes, can only be a positive step.

Custody is very much at the heart of our work in divorce mediation, and it's often an extremely difficult question. It's hard to work through the overlay of emotions, rationalizations, grief, and anguish and see who these people really are and what it is they really want. But our point is certainly to prevent further deterioration of the child. I would say that mediation allows the child the best possible chance.

EIGHT

Learning from Our Mistakes

Only four of the scores of women with whom we talked had actually known any other woman who had made this choice. The action was totally outside the realm of their experience. Even those who did know another woman in this situation didn't necessarily find it a positive example.

Past Experience

My aunt had given up her children many years ago, and I guess on some level I always thought she was a selfish woman. And it's true that she is, whether she had her children or not. Now I think she may have done the best thing—her husband was obviously the better parent, and I think she knew that. Her children have grown up beautifully. But I didn't know that when I first heard about it. I didn't think too highly of her.

There was someone on my mother's side of the family who was a real mystery person. I knew she existed, but I could never find out anything about her, and of course that made me all the more fascinated. No one liked to talk about her, and when they did everything they said was a lie. They all told the story that they had agreed on years ago. Well, eventually I found out what it was all about: she had left her children with their father. It was evident what everyone in the family thought about this. They tried to pretend she didn't exist.

I knew a woman who left her kids and moved away, and she was a real flake. She just reinforced the stereotype of the abandoning mother for me. She was selfish, unthinking, unstable, and she really did, more or less, abandon her kids although their father took care of them. So when I began to consider the possibility of living without my kids I certainly didn't identify with her, but I wondered if other people would see me that way.

I met someone who had done this six years ago, and I was excited to talk to her about it. But she was very peculiar and refused to discuss it at all.

Hindsights

Struggling through this difficult process without models or guidelines, most women feel that they make mistakes, sometimes substantial ones. These may be tactical errors, errors of judgment, or a woman may simply have a sense of not having handled things as well as she might have. If they had it to do over again, we asked our interviewees, knowing what they know now, how would they do things differently? It was rare to hear an interviewee respond that she was thoroughly pleased with her performance and satisfied that she had done the best she could. Even women who were extremely pleased with the results of their decisions felt that they could have dealt with making those decisions more effectively.

I made so many mistakes. I blundered through the whole thing. Even with good motives and being conscientious and trying to do the best I could and being in therapy throughout, I still made terrible mistakes that I wish I could correct.

My guilt now is not that I'm not residing with the children but that I made so many mistakes in the process of taking that step. I made so many mistakes handling it all. I just wasn't very aware of the intellectual and psychic dynamics of the situation, for me or for my kids. I simply wasn't that aware of myself and my own responses.

It's worked out very well, but I'm amazed by that. Looking back, it seems to me I did so many things wrong. I'd handle it in a very different way today, but thank God human beings are resilient. I guess my mistakes didn't do any permanent damage.

The Stress—and Distress—of Divorce

Divorce is enormously stressful. Studies have shown that at the time of divorce a mother's and father's parenting abilities suffer as a consequence of the parents' absorption in their own distress. Women who separate from their children at the time of divorce may realize, after the fact, how little they were able to consider the children at the time of the decision and regret that enormously.

At the time of the separation if my husband had said, "I'll take all the money, all the property, and the children, and I'll shoot you," I would have said, "Uh-huh. Okay." I was in such a state I couldn't even communicate with my lawyer. He was the best lawyer money could buy, but he couldn't stand to see me cry. I feel if I'd gotten the woman lawyer I have now at the very beginning, I might now be in a very different position. But I couldn't think clearly, about myself, about the kids, about anything.

I regret that I didn't have some time to myself to get my mind together, just some space to get away for a while to think. Maybe if I could have done that and have had the children stay with someone I could rely on and then come back with a clear head, then maybe I could have tolerated it and coped. But I was really at the end of my rope, and I know I thought my husband would be the best one to raise the children.

What I didn't realize of course was that he would turn around and be as mean as he was about letting me see them. I kept thinking that if I had them I'd be going out of my way to see that they kept in contact with their dad. But I guess what happened was that he thought if he had the kids, I'd come back to him, and when I didn't that really took the wind out of his sails, and he became very vindictive.

I wish I'd been more pulled together at that time. I wish I'd thought or even known of the words joint custody. *And I wish I could have stricken the phrase* reasonable rights of visitation *from my divorce decree because I found out that in a divorce there are no reasonable people.*

I don't think I understood enough the impact on the children. I thought it wouldn't make any difference that I was the one to leave. But now I think it does make a difference because of our society. At the time I didn't really look at it from a social standpoint.

My kids don't know anyone else whose mother has left the house. In our society mothers don't leave, and if you're going to live in this world you've got to live by the rules, whether you like it or not, and that's one of the rules. This way my kids are not only dealing with the divorce but with outside pressures. I thought too much about how I'd react, not how my kids would. I didn't think they'd blame me so much.

If I had it to do over again I'd be much more attentive to my kids and aware of how hard all this was on them. Of course I knew it was affecting them, and I tried to reassure them and to let them know that I was still their mother no matter where I was living. But I don't think I did enough of that. I was so caught up in my own struggle to make this decision that I'm afraid they sort of got the short end of the stick.

Cumulative Guilt

A few women, in the immediate aftermath of divorce and separation from their children, stayed away altogether for a time. Guilty about leaving their kids in the first place, they avoided them as reminders of that guilt. The longer they stayed away, of course, the worse the guilt became.

It may be easier for the mother not to be in contact with the child for a while, but I think it's always best for the child to be in contact with the mother. And I'd have to go with the child. I guess it's the old statement from Guess Who's Coming to Dinner?*: the child didn't* *ask to be born but the child is there, and it's the adult's responsibility to provide some stability for the child and not totally disappear out of the child's life.*

Now I can't imagine it, but I just took off. I'd never do such a thing if I were in that position today. I just couldn't deal with any of it. And of course the longer I stayed away, the more ashamed I felt.

Women who completely absent themselves from their children may carry the heaviest burden of guilt in later years. Often these are young, rather immature, women who committed themselves early to marriages in which they later felt trapped. Bolting from their marriages and from their children as well, they had few coping skills and little ability to think beyond their own dissatisfaction and frustration. Yet as they grow up and acquire a more mature perspective, they may come to regret deeply their earlier behavior. They may then wish to reestablish closeness with their children but find that it is very difficult to do so. Conversely, the women who behave most responsibly in this difficult and hurtful situation tend to suffer fewer regrets and less inner guilt.

Out of Touch

You'd think I would have been more careful since I grew up in a situation where I felt my parents more or less abandoned me. They were always involved in their own struggles. But when my marriage broke up I just took off and left my son behind. I didn't even stop to consider him really, and I loved him.

But that was the wrong move. I lost him. I was so emotionally uptight at the time. It worked out okay ultimately, and I think it was probably in my child's best interests that he was where he was, but it just seems I could have figured out something better. I just could have handled it better.

My daughter was living in the West with her father and stepmother, and I had moved to the East, and at one point she was supposed to come for a visit. I'd saved and saved for this because my ex-husband wouldn't help me out with traveling money. Then I got sick and lost my job and the money went, and he still wouldn't help me out so that she could come. I said, "All right, if that's the way it is, you'll never hear from me again." I was very bitter, and I just decided to withdraw. I felt the stepmother wanted that. I felt she wanted to erase me. She didn't want me in the way, and so I thought maybe that's the way it's supposed to be. I didn't want to break up their family. I decided I wouldn't meddle with it. I didn't see my daughter for four years.

When the time came that I did see her, it wasn't easy to become acquainted again. It was very strange for us to be together and we were both very nervous about it. It would have been better if we'd never been out of contact like we were, but I didn't know that at the time I broke off the contact.

I needed some space. I didn't want to be responsible for anyone or anything. I just wanted to go away for a little while. And my husband said to me I could never have my son back if I left. My son was four at the time. So I knew what the score was, but I left anyway. I wasn't mature enough then to have a child.

There was a period of about two years where I didn't see my child, and during that time I grew up. I had a breakdown. I couldn't stop crying. But I had a therapist and a good friend who saved my life. Now I do see my son again, and when I'm with him I try to really devote myself to him and listen to what he has to say and do things he likes to do. I figure I took my time for myself and he deserves to have his time. I've told him I'll never let him down again.

Living Proof

One very difficult thing for women in this situation to achieve is clarity about their motives. The culture deems it unacceptable for a woman to "give up" her children. So many women find it impossible to acknowledge that that is what they want. This necessity to mask their own desires may be operating in some of the instances in which women accept custody following the divorce but then relinquish it later. Sometimes this is a woman's way of *proving* that it is untenable for her to be a single parent. In fact, the situation might have been better for everyone if the children had lived with their father immediately following the divorce.

I wish I'd been seeing a therapist when I was in the middle of all that. I wish I'd been talking things out. As it was, I really didn't understand what was going on. I didn't know what I wanted and what I didn't. I was in a fog.

It's really important to examine why you're doing this. The first thing to ask is if you're sending your child to the father out of anger. That's not good if you are. But maybe, instead, in the long run you think it will be best for both of you. And then you have to ask, what kind of family is he going to? Then, after that, you have to ask, how can I deal with being a part-time mother? How can I deal with giving my son's life over to another woman? And you have to be prepared for the child to be angry. You have to be able to explain that you're not deserting him, that you'll be there.

What I'm saying is that it's important to take the time to look at all these questions. And it's not always easy to answer them honestly, but it's important to try. I have to be willing to own up to the fact that I like being alone, I like my freedom as well as the fact that I think it's good for my son to be with his father at this point in his life.

I kept my kids for about six months after the divorce, and then I thought I'd really go nuts. There was just no way I could go on juggling everything and not go crazy. I really felt stretched to the breaking point. With three kids, just trying to keep up with the daily chores and meals and so on can make you feel that way. But I was working too, and it was really impossible. I never should have taken them in the first place. Their father wanted them, but I insisted they had to be with me. It wasn't a good idea. It took the kids and me about a year to recover from that.

Making It Clear to the Kids

Several women said they regretted not dealing more straightforwardly with their children about their decision. They felt, with hindsight, that they could have given the children more reassurance about the future.

We didn't deal honestly enough with the kids. There wasn't enough talk beforehand between us about the decision, and there wasn't enough talk with them once we had made the decision. We should have had counseling. That would have helped. We should have tried to talk more. But, of course, that's what ruined our marriage. We never talked.

We should have done more explaining to our kids. We should have given them more assurance about what was going to be happening. I just recently heard about something called a service of affirmation, and that really made sense to me because it emphasized that both parents will still go on being parents even though they no longer love each other. I'm not sure we made that clear enough to our kids.

Co-parenting

The service referred to above is one of the "divorce ceremonies" the clergy has been developing in recent years to mark the major change in life that divorce represents. The children are present at this service of affirmation in which the parents absolve the children of any blame for their separation and commit themselves to continuing to be responsible, loving parents, cooperating with each other in that endeavor.

Cooperation and communication between ex-spouses on matters of child-rearing is often a troublesome area. Here, also, parents are not always able to put the child's interests first. Their own need to punish their ex-mate may supersede their concern for the child's welfare. But no one will suffer as acutely as a child who constantly witnesses parental conflict. Many women we interviewed said that communication with their ex-husbands was the most problematic aspect of their present living arrangement. This was sometimes true even when the mother and father had joint custody.

It really has worked out wonderfully. With my life the way it is I think we arrived at the best arrangement. I wouldn't have much time for my kids during the week if they lived with me, so it's better that I spend weekends with them. And my husband has also undergone a tremendous metamorphosis. He's become very domestic and really thrown himself into it and made a big effort. My only complaint at present is that I'd like a little better relationship with him regarding the children. He doesn't like to talk to me about anything. He simply doesn't want to relate to me.

We still have a battle over co-parenting. It's been awful. I don't want an armed camp. I don't want my kids involved in that. But I just hate what I see as his heavy duty programming of them. I'm afraid that they'll become part of the American dream machine as defined by their father before they can ever become free of it and make their own decisions.

I've gotten used to the idea that I'm not in on the day-to-day decisions, but there are ways in which I'd like to be more involved with my kids. For instance, I've asked to see copies of their report cards, but their father just refuses. I've asked to see copies of psychological reports on my son who has learning disabilities, but he's also refused to show me those.

My ex-husband constantly accuses me of interfering with the housekeepers he hires, and he insists that's why he's lost so many of them. Well, if that's true then I've done it unwittingly. What I have *done is to make sure that if he's out of town the housekeepers can call and ask me any questions they might have. I've done this because he forgets things. He'll do things like leave and go away on a trip without giving the housekeeper a note so that she could get the kids treated at a hospital if she needed to. Those are the kind of things he overlooks.*

Our separation was rather amicable for the first six months or so, but it's been downhill ever since then. He has continued to be a good father, but our relationship has slowly deteriorated to almost nonspeaking terms. Now he's like a possessed man, determined to make my life miserable. I think he's in a rage that I've defied him. That of course creates problems for the children. The only difficulty I ever have with them now is when I try to appeal to them to help make sure that I see them at certain times. I'm in some sense appealing for their help in dealing with their father. But they don't want to hear it. They just say, "Don't start, Mother." I live thousands of miles away from them, and I wish they were closer to me, but I wouldn't want to live one inch closer to that man.

I have to be very devious with my ex-husband to get what I want for my children. If I say X, he does Y. I think he'll always do the opposite of what he thinks I want. Anything I want he's determined I'm not going to get it. I want them to go to camp next summer, but if I say that to him, there's no way they'll get a chance to go.

As soon as the kids went to live with my ex-husband, he turned on me and tried to get the kids to see me with a negative image. He wouldn't communicate with me. He said to me once, "I wouldn't drive them to the end of the driveway to see you." And that's just about how cooperative he's been ever since.

As soon as I became financially independent of my ex-husband he began playing games. He gives me trouble about their visitation time, comes up with various problems about this and that, reasons they can't arrive when they should or stay as long as they might. He's causing problems for me that I shouldn't have and asking questions I shouldn't have to answer. It's getting very sticky, and I'm afraid I'm going to have to have a lawyer intervene. I'm sort of terrified of facing that whole scene, but I think I'm going to have to.

Some women reported that they had quite amicable, cooperative relationships with their ex-husbands in regard to their children. A few said this had occurred easily, naturally. Others stressed that it took a great deal of work to maintain a certain level of cooperation. All of them mentioned how important they felt it was for their children's welfare.

I don't like my husband as a husband, but as a parent he's first-rate. Things between us are pretty cordial, although right now I'm somewhat suspicious of his new wife's relationship to my son. He says she yells at him when his father isn't there, and she's really great to him when his father is there. I talked to my ex-husband about this, and he confirmed my suspicions and promised to deal with the situation, and I'm confident that he will.

I simply refuse to be my ex's enemy. I can't afford that for my son's sake. What if this situation had come up and my son's father and I were barely speaking? I wouldn't have been able to do anything about it. I wouldn't have been able to help my son. Our relationship must remain as civilized as we can possibly make it for our child's sake.

Both my ex and I may have had occasional rivalries or feelings of jealousy, but our son seems to have balanced all that so well. When he lived with his father he wanted to see me every weekend and vice versa. I suppose that both my ex and I have occasionally slandered each other but not obsessively and not with a great investment in it. And I know our son doesn't want to hear it. He doesn't pay much attention to the judgments when I do do it.

Basically his father and I have a lot of respect for each other as parents. We basically agree on most stuff in the parenting area. My son and his father really enjoy being with each other, and both my ex and I have made it easy for each other to keep the bond with our son. I'd always make sure that he'd see his father and work my schedule around that. I'm very supportive of their spending time together, and he's done the same for me. I think we were much more eager for our son to have a relationship with each of us than we were to be the favorite.

We have a very good working relationship when it comes to the kids. And at the time of the divorce I tried to build up my husband to the kids. I didn't tell them negative things about him. I just said we were very different people. A child contains both parents, and if you put down one parent, you're putting down something that lives within that child; you're diminishing a part of your own child.

I wanted to think of this whole process as a reorganization of family life, not the destruction of it. I wasn't angry with my husband. I just wanted out of a life-style that was incompatible with my needs. I tried all the way through to think how can we diffuse this, move past that, avoid bloodshed—and it worked.

There's a lot of day-to-day stuff that I disagree with in my kids' life with their father, like eating habits, both adults in the house smoking, stuff like that. But any important decisions to do with the kids my husband discusses with me. I consider him a good friend, a close friend.

We always agreed from the beginning of our marriage that we would have a united front when it came to the children. And we've always stuck to that, even though we're separated and one of the kids is now living with him.

You have to stay in contact and stay flexible. This is a situation that changes all the time. You have to play it by ear and check all the time, check the reality to see how the children are doing. Change it if you have to. And you have to support each other. Whoever has the child needs the support of the other parent. Make it a joint effort if you can. I have to say I think we've been model parents. We've really worked at it—we've worked hard—and I think it will reflect in our daughter for the rest of her life.

My kids have been through enough without having to watch me and their father carve each other up. There are times I've really felt like going after him on something, but I won't do it. He and I can just put aside our own animosities and work together to make the situation as good for the kids as it can be. We couldn't stay together for them, but we can give them that.

Besides that, it's just practical to maintain good relations with your ex-husband. You have a lot better chance of getting what you want for your children if the two of you are speaking to each other.

The Fight to Stay Friends

Occasionally, however, the effort to maintain amicability with an ex-mate can become an excuse. A woman who is afraid to assert herself, afraid to make demands regarding her children, may believe that her unwillingness to argue is part of fostering friendly relations between her and her ex-husband. The reality is that sometimes conflict is necessary and peace at any price can be harmful. If a mother is not forceful in stating her needs vis-a-vis her children, the reality is that she may end up not seeing them very often and perhaps lose touch with them entirely.

My question now is whether or not I want to antagonize my husband over details—should I have the kids one month or two in the summer, see them every other weekend or every third weekend? It's my understanding that if you can establish a good relationship with your ex that the legal details often go by the boards, and then you can work out what's best for everyone. I don't want to put him off, but he's adamant that I only have the children for one month in the summer.

I've just gotten a new lawyer, and she was shocked when I told her what limited access I was going to have to the children. I asked her if I might get more in terms of the children by giving up some of my demands about property and alimony and so on. I can fight over the money and the property, but when it comes to the children I lose my fight. I'm so demoralized by it. I'm angry at being in a situation where I have to fight to be part of my children's lives. And I'm also angry that I'm not fighting. I don't deserve to be shut out of their lives. I feel it's all beneath me, this fighting. It shouldn't be occurring. I shouldn't have to devote myself to this.

My husband changed his unlisted number to another unlisted number, so now I can't even call my children. He does outrageous things like this, but I still don't want to interfere with him because I don't want his rage, and I don't want it spilling over onto the children. I try to do everything I can to keep friction at a minimum. But I'm afraid to confront him, even with this thing about the telephone. I'm afraid of his rage.

Getting Out Late

Several women we interviewed expressed regret that they had not left their marriages sooner. In most instances, these were marriages that were bad from the beginning, but the women stayed out of fear and dependency. When they did finally leave, their resources were often severely depleted. They had no money, no skills, no self-esteem, and no ability to make responsible and sensible decisions.

There were two reasons I got married. One was that I felt like there wasn't anything else to do. The other was that I slept with my boyfriend when I was sixteen, and he convinced me that that was the end of my life, that no one else would ever have me because I wasn't a virgin. This was in the 1950s and I'd read Marjorie Morningstar *and I knew what happened to her. And she was gorgeous and rich and even so he wouldn't have her, so I knew my boyfriend was right and I married him. Well, nine years later I left him because I finally realized that things would never be better or different and that my life was in my own hands, and if I didn't do something about it, nothing was going to get done. But I really regret not getting out sooner. Maybe I wouldn't have been so desperate.*

As it was, what I did was just take the kids and flee without telling him anything. I was terribly guilty. First, I was guilty because I felt I wasn't really doing enough for my kids. We'd gone from a nice house in a neighborhood they liked to a small apartment. We'd gone from having plenty of money to never having enough. And I was guilty because I felt it was a mistake to have taken them away from him.

They had been really unhappy with a lot of what was going on with him. He and I fought a lot, and that was hard on the children. He would scream and yell. He was very domineering, and sometimes he was very rough on the children as well. He'd go on rampages and really drive them to distraction, insisting they do certain things. But once we were away from him they didn't remember a lot of that. Once a bad situation is behind you, you can quickly forget a lot of it.

So as soon as we left him, they were torn. They knew he wanted them with him, and they felt guilty about being with me. Eventually he got them back, of course. But in the meantime it was hard on everyone. And if I'd left sooner maybe all that wouldn't have happened.

I remember once fairly early in my marriage going to our family doctor for advice because I was so unhappy. He said to me, "Look, you've got your life. You've made it. Get yourself some women friends, go to lunch, go shopping, take in an early movie, take care of your child and make your life." I finally said, help, I'm miserable, *and this is what I got.*

By the time my ex and I separated, I felt like I didn't want anything to do with any part of that marriage, and for a while that included my kids, I guess. We had three kids, and I'd raised them alone and been with them twenty-four hours a day for more than eight years, and all I wanted when I left was distance. The marriage was so awful and I was so wrung out from fighting my way through it that I felt like I didn't have anything to give anyone. And I didn't. I was really a mess.

I really had to sort of rebuild myself before I could establish a relationship with my kids, and today I've done that. But it took a lot of time and a lot of healing before I could do it. Maybe if I hadn't hung in on the marriage so long I wouldn't have so totally lost sight of who I was. I just feel I completely lost myself for a while there.

Looking back, I see things differently from how I saw them then. I had expected that my ex-husband would form a closer relationship with the kids once I was out of the way. But that didn't happen. He remarried and he didn't do as much directly with the kids as you'd expect he would. After the breakup he identified the kids with me, as did their stepmother.

I had initiated the idea of the kids staying with him because I didn't want to uproot them, and I thought he was a good father. But I've changed my mind about that. And I think my kids wish now that they had been more aggressive in expressing themselves about what was happening. They thought the matter was all settled and that there wasn't any room for their input. They might have helped to reach an alternative solution. I don't know.

At the time I left, my kids were sixteen, fifteen, and thirteen, girls with a boy in the middle. They were happy living where they were, and I thought the situation was solved in the best way for them. For myself, however, I think I should have left the marriage sooner, and if I had, I would have taken them with me.

Could It Have Lasted?

A few women expressed regret that they had not worked harder at their marriages; if their behavior had been different the marriages might have lasted.

When I look back now I see that I could have been more forceful. I wouldn't have asked for certain things; I would have demanded them. And if I'd done that a lot of the problems we'd had might never have come up. I would have demanded that I hold a job or that we move to the city. And other things I might have tried to see his way. One huge bone of contention between us was to get someone good to stay with the children when I traveled with him. He always refused to pay the rate the agencies were asking. So if he wouldn't pay, I wouldn't go. I could have been more flexible about that. If I had it to do over, I'd work harder at the marriage because I see now how important a relationship is and how hard you have to work at it.

I think I could have worked harder to keep the marriage together. this thing of staying together for the children isn't all wrong. But I wouldn't go back now—and he wouldn't take me back

Rating Him As a Father

A cautionary note was sounded by some of the women we interviewed with regard to their ex-husband's qualities as fathers. Some felt they should have given this greater weight in making a decision about where the children should live. Others were convinced that their decision had been sound but regretted the influence of their ex-husband's personality on their children.

Make sure you look into your husband's qualities very carefully before you leave your children with him. Be sure he has a relationship with the children that goes beyond just lord of the manor. Be sure he takes a personal, down-to-earth interest in them. Not: "Oh, you want to play football? Okay, I'll get you all the best equipment and I'll be the coach and why didn't you do better?" Make sure he can really communicate and enjoy the children and laugh with them. I see now how important that is, that laughter. I laugh over things with them now that I wouldn't have laughed at if I was living with them. And I wonder why I didn't do that more often.

I saw my kids very little while they were growing up, and I have a lot of regrets about that. I'm sorry now that I didn't have a greater role in bringing them up because I see how they've grown up, and I disagree with so many of the things my ex-husband has done with them. Basically they're wonderful children, and that has to do with the fact that he really loves them. But they spend a lot of time watching TV and eating spaghetti and drinking soda. It's just a very different sensibility from mine. I wish they'd had a little more inspiration in their lives.

I didn't pay enough attention to my ex-husband's qualities as a parent when I made my decision. I was quite focused on my own needs, and I'm not sure that was all wrong. But the main thing I knew at the time was that he loved them, and that seemed like enough. Then we separated and he was quite bitter and explosive for a while, and that really was not good for the children. He got so caught up in his anger at me that he couldn't pay all that much attention to them. I hadn't anticipated that.

Now that some time has passed things are better, but I still see that my ex-husband is not who I thought he was. I still have no doubt that he loves his kids, but I'm not sure anymore that just love is enough to make you a good parent.

I considered my ex-husband a good father. He wasn't afraid to be affectionate. He was very outdoorsy, into all those activities, and we had two sons, so that seemed like it was good. But the only thing that bothers me now is that I find them inhibited. They used to be very uninhibited and creative and daring. One, in particular, is quite withdrawn now, and he used to be very outgoing, and I wonder if his father has broken his spirit.

The thing that's so hard about this is that your kids become extensions of this spouse you don't like. If you liked him you'd still be together. There were qualities I really liked in my kids that I've seen change.

In some areas my ex-husband is very strong, a very good father. but in some areas he's very empty. You can't talk about feelings with him.

One woman whose children had been snatched by her ex-husband—who then made it clear that the children themselves preferred to *stay* with him—felt that she had acceded to certain specific legalities too quickly. The situation was agonizing to her, and she wanted simply to end the conflict.

The whole thing was very traumatic for the children, as well as for me, even if they did prefer to live with him. There was a period where I didn't see them at all, and whenever I did he'd convinced them that I would try to kidnap them back. It was awful and once I'd gone through this horrible anguish and decided to let them stay with him, I just wanted to get it over with. I was too quick to agree to seeing them every three weeks. I wish I'd insisted on every second weekend. I also guess I could have given their living with him a trial period rather than giving up custody. But he would have fought that, and I just couldn't battle in court with him. I was in no condition for that. I just wanted it settled.

Taking a Stronger Stand

The issue of proximity to the children was an important one for many women. Those mothers who lived near their children and saw them frequently were involved in their children's lives in a way that wasn't possible for mothers who lived at a distance. Most of the latter expressed regret and recognized what they were missing by not having more frequent contact wth their children. Some of them said that they wished they had taken a stronger stand on the issue when it first arose.

When my husband said that he and the kids were moving across the country I knew it would be difficult, but I had no idea how difficult. If it happened today I'd say, absoutely not. *And I had the legal right to say that at the time. But he threatened me with court, and I was terrified of that. Now if it came up I'd go to court even though I'm still opposed to the court being involved in this. It just doesn't seem like the right place to settle these things.*

What's different now is that I know that the distance is just as traumatic as a court battle would have been. When we lived together in the same city it was great; we really shared the kids. The worst mistake I made in this whole thing was letting him take the kids three thousand miles away. It's consistently painful to me.

Sometimes the distance needn't be great to cause problems.

Our divorce agreement says we mustn't live more than twenty-five miles apart, but my ex-husband recently moved about fifty miles away. It doesn't seem like much, but it's created a really big hassle. Because of the way public transportation is set up, I now have to travel seven hours to pick my son up and take him back to his father. That makes it just that much harder to see him, and we don't have so much time together. A big part of it is spent traveling.

Difficult to Watch

The process of redefining oneself is rarely tidy. Many women we interviewed had married young, going directly from their parents' home into marriage, exchanging the role of daughter for the role of wife/mother. When the time of divorce came and they shed the role of full-time mother as well, they felt adrift. They began only then to discover who they really were, apart from their roles. They asked questions, they floundered around, they struggled, and it was sometimes quite chaotic.

It is a difficult thing for a child to watch a parent go through this sort of distress and confusion, and several women regretted not having shielded their children more thoroughly. Some of these same women noted that during this period of conflict they had put their kids in inappropriate positions, such as confidante or pal. They had placed their own needs before the need of a child to have a strong and stable parental figure.

I was just discovering that I was gay, and I handled that very badly. I was very naïve. My daughter was only ten, but I was honest with her about this—I was honest with everybody. Well, I wouldn't necessarily advocate that today. Honesty is not *always the best policy. She felt no stability with me; she felt she couldn't count on me. I seemed to be a totally other person than the one she'd always known. It was a very upsetting time, and I was acting out all over the place, exhibiting my lesbianism, making "my statement," take it or leave it. I just went through a whole thing, and she felt that suddenly she was seeing a complete stranger.*

I understand now that that must have been awful for her. At the time I thought, I'm making my statement, and she'll understand later on. Well, I don't see it that way now. I wouldn't need to do that today. I can see it from her point of view now, and what it meant to her was that she couldn't count on the mother that she had known.

When my daughter first lived with her father she lived downtown with him, and I lived uptown. She got in with a Rocky Horror group, and the first few times she asked me to come with her, and I did. I have a feeling for kids, and I knew all her friends. We became pals for a time, which was not a good idea, I discovered. You're not supposed to be your kid's pal. You're supposed to be the parent. I think my guilt that she wasn't living with me made me try to be her pal. Now I'm trying to get back to being a parent.

I think for a while I treated my kids, especially my oldest daughter, like best friends, and I'm really sorry that I did that. I see what a burden it placed on them. They would come to me for a weekend and I'd just pour out everything, things they had no business knowing, things that could have been very upsetting for them. I treated them like they were the points of stability in my world. I depended on them for some sense of continuity about myself. And it should have been the other way around.

Nearly all the many, many women we talked with felt they had made the right decision even though most of them had regrets about how they had handled certain things. Over and over again they expressed their conviction that it also had proved to be the best decision for everyone involved. They recognized that their present arrangement had flaws. Most wished for some aspect of the situation to be changed: better communication with their children's father; more opportunities to see the children; a greater sense of meaningful input in their children's lives; a deeper level of acceptance of the decision within themselves. But still they felt it was the most viable arrangement for all concerned. Only one woman we talked with was actively considering going to court to reverse her present custody situation. Only one woman said she regretted her decision altogether. Asked what she might say that could be helpful to other women in this situation, she answered unhelpfully, "Just don't give them up." Only one other woman was truly uncertain as to whether or not she had done the right thing.

I was a mess. There's no other way to put it. I was full of turmoil and conflict, and the kids were giving me a hard time, and my husband was pressuring me. But when I finally gave in to his pressure I really did it without a lot of thought, and I've regretted that. When I hear now of women doing this I tell them they might be sorry. I tell them to be sure to think it through very carefully.

I've been without my kids for ten years now, and it's only in the last year and a half that I've discovered what it is I really like and want to do, and I'm working hard at it. If I'd stayed where I was I never would have discovered that; I'd never have had the life I have. What I've decided recently is that I'm sorry but I'm not sorry.

Support Systems

As noted, most women went through the process of separating from their children without a strong sense of support and assistance. They went through all the difficult feelings they have described essentially alone. And that isolation only fed their sense of self-doubt and self-recrimination. Additionally, deprived as they were of any forum for discussion, they often remained in the dark, or at least confused, about their own needs and wants.

Those women who were receiving some sort of therapy while they were making the decision to live apart from their children did seem to have a somewhat easier time of it. They were able to understand themselves, their actions, and their reactions more fully because they were able to examine those things in a safe environment, free of condemnation and censure. Those women who did not receive professional counseling but had the understanding and fellowship of a few close friends found their burden was lightened considerably by being able to verbalize their feelings and explore their options with a sympathetic listener.

As we know, any woman making this choice, or considering it, needs all the help she can get. Society itself offers little in this regard. It is generally up to the woman herself to take the responsibility for generating and developing her own support network. And it is extremely important to do so.

One woman we interviewed addressed herself to her own need for support on a truly grand scale. She was living in Europe at the time of her divorce and separation from her children.

> *I started a group for women in this situation when I found that there wasn't one. I wrote a letter to the national newspaper, saying that I was a woman separated from her children and aware of the stigma associated with that, and I said I was willing to talk to other women in this situation with the hope that we could share and support each other. At that time, from that single letter, I heard from five hundred women, and we started a group that eventually became MATCH (Mothers Apart From Their Children). That became the most important thing I've ever done in my life.*
>
> *I became close friends with the women the group attracted, and meeting other women and sharing our experience had an almost cathartic effect. It started the healing process. It was good for me in every way: intellectually stimulating, emotionally rewarding, and very growthful for me personally and professionally.*

Obviously, initiating an enterprise of this nature would not be the answer for every woman. But on a much smaller scale women can reap some of the same sort of rewards by making sure they surround themselves with positive, caring friends. And there is an existing group, the recently established Mothers Without Children, that brings together women in this situation to share their experiences.

When we asked our interviewees what advice they would give to any woman considering this option, many of them mentioned the matter of support in one way or another. Those who had had it recognized how important, how crucial, it had been. Those who had been without it knew what they had missed.

> *I'd say to any mother thinking about this that before she makes the move, she should develop a support system for herself because she's going to need it—not only for the negative feelings about giving up the children but also for the positive ones as well. The most difficult things are saying, "I'm thirty-six and I'm free, and maybe I can start to live my life and find out who I am." That's the most difficult part of the whole thing, the most guilt-producing. The positive feelings are the ones that haunt you most.*

Hearing from the Kids

We also interviewed some of the children of the women who have spoken throughout this book. These interviews were necessarily more limited in number and scope, but we did discover that most of the children were pleased with their present living arrangements and felt, on balance, that living with their fathers had been the best choice for them. If they were living at some distance from their mothers, the children expressed a wish that she were closer. Those whose fathers had remarried said that they liked the feeling of being in a family situation. "It's better when it's not just a mom and two kids." is the way one eleven-year-old boy put it. All of the children mentioned an improved relationship with the mother now that they were living apart from her.

But even though they were pleased by the outcome, most had complaints about how their parents had handled the whole custody matter, and they also had advice to give to other children and to parents finding themselves in this situation. Two of the common threads in the advice were that the children be given more respect in this process and that the children themselves attempt to exert as much influence as possible on their own behalf.

Both of those threads are evident in the excerpts that follow from an interview with a seventeen-year-old girl who has lived with her father for several years. When her parents divorced she was eleven and her brother was three. Her mother, who lives in an eastern city, lived with the children following the divorce. Two years later, while retaining joint custody, she let the children go to live with their father. He moved to the West Coast soon afterward.

Before the divorce I was closer to my mother, and I never really talked much to my dad. I think she was bored with being just a wife and a mother, but she did have time for me. Then, after the divorce, she became very unpredictable. She was trying to get her life together and going to school, and she was really uptight because of studying and the money situation. She didn't have much money or much time for us. Her main objective was to be able to support herself, and she was working really hard toward that. Everybody was tense all the time. Anything that happened, she blew up and became angry. There was just a lot of tension. I understand why, but I still don't think it was justified.

My parents asked me then who I'd rather live with, and I couldn't answer that. It just made me feel pressured. There were pros and cons on each side, and I just left it up to them. So the decision was made for us to go with our father, and it was better for us because he had more money, and I could have nice clothes and a regular allowance and a lot of freedom once we moved out West. That move was good for me and my brother. It was a positive step. Living in the city wasn't doing anything for me; if anything, it was bringing me down. I had some really hard years there when I was on pretty shaky ground. I was just going day to day. But things have been more settled since we moved. I have more concern for my future. I'm starting to think about what I want to do. I have more freedom, more independence. I think it was a better choice to live with my father.

I know now that parents are real people, not just Mom and Dad. They're not always going to be there to take care of me. Things happen. Things change. There was a time when I didn't feel that I could count on either one of them, although I do now. I feel that neither parent was there for me for a time. They put their lives first, their careers. My mother did it to be able to support herself and to be happy with what she's doing. My father's just a very hard worker. He just works all the time. I think they could have taken a little more time out for me. I think they could have had time for me and for their own lives too. It hurt my feelings, though I wasn't conscious of it at the time.

I didn't really talk to anyone while I was going through this. Friends would listen but they didn't really know what it was like. This was some time ago, and I think people are more understanding now because it's much more common. They don't look down on you anymore as an abandoned child. It's not as shocking as it used to be. Two of my close friends now are in the same situation.

I learned something very positive from my mother: that if you're in a situation where you're not happy, you can always change it. You always have a choice. You don't have to be stuck with one thing for the rest of your life. But I think she could have gone about making the change in a different way. I think in the process of making the change you can try to be considerate of the children. And perhaps before making the decision, give it a little more thought. I think my mother did try to talk to me, but I was too young to understand. All I knew was that my safe, protected life was just being turned upside down.

I'd say to any child in this situation: put yourself first. Weigh things out carefully and see which situation, living with your father or your mother, is going to be better for you. Don't necessarily just go by who you get along with best or who you've always talked to most. You have to weigh everything.

I have a lot of resentment about all this, but I can't keep bringing up the past. Everyone was hurt in their own way by what we went through. But you have to look ahead. You can't look back.

I guess I don't show either of my parents that I'd like to spend more time with them. I just recently talked about this with my father, and we decided we'd go out together one night a week. I feel good about that; we should have done it a long time ago. It's hard to be so far away from my mother. I can't just call her up and say, "Let's meet for lunch." But I think the time we do spend together is pretty close now. It's the one thing I don't like about where I live. I'd like her to be closer. I wish she'd move here. Now I feel it's time that people started coming to me—I've moved around a lot.

NINE

Summing Up

I had nothing to read, nobody to talk to. I felt I was making a truly pioneer step. It was terribly frightening. I had no models. Even good therapists I knew hadn't had experience with this. So I began thinking on my own; what, in fact, is it to be a good mother? I couldn't reconcile my idea of who I was with not being a good mother. Is being a good mother baking chocolate chip cookies? Is it doing gymnastics and karate classes? Is it getting your children up for school, feeding them, cooking for them?

And then I began to think anout the highest quality relationships that I have with my friends. None of these are based on any of these tasks or services. Rather, they're based on the quality of intimacy we've been able to establish and a kind of sharing of our development as people.

What is it to be a good mother? It is not a question to which there are any easy or painless answers. But pieces of answers have become clear in the course of this book. A woman who elects to put her own needs first may be doing the right thing for her entire family. A woman who is physically separated from her children some of the time may end up being more emotionally present for them all the time. These assertions contradict our old notions of motherhood. Yet all of them are based on the experience of women who have moved beyond those old notions and tried something new.

Best for Everyone

I remember very clearly having the sense that I was entering uncharted territory, having the sense that no one had been here before me. And I certainly stumbled and fumbled because of that, the path wasn't marked and I had to find my own way. When there's nothing to hold yourself up against it raises a lot of questions, and I asked all of them. What sort of person was I? What did this choice say about me? Was I rationalizing? Was I being honest? How would my kids be affected? Could I go ahead and do this without knowing the answer to that question?

*It's a monumental task to go against your conditioning, and of course you pay a price for it. But as time passed and I struggled with these questions, the decision just came to seem more and more inevitable. I knew it was the right one for me, and I believed—*I believed—*that it would end up being the best for everyone else as well. Of course I questioned that belief. Was that simply what I wanted to believe? Was I throwing myself a sop—ultimately it will be best for everyone—just so I'd be able to make the move?*

I still don't know the answers to those questions, but they don't seem so important now because it really has worked out well. It has *been best for everyone. I'm convinced of that.*

I expected other people to give me trouble with this, but I had no idea how much trouble I'd give myself. This choice absolutely contradicted everything I'd been taught, everything I'd observed all my life. I knew what a mother was and what she wasn't. And one thing she certainly wasn't was someone who'd choose to live without her children. Yet I felt I was a good mother, and I knew I loved my children very much. What I'm saying is that it felt like a very revolutionary act to me, but I went ahead and did it anyway. Despite everything else, I knew what I felt inside meant I'd continue to be a good mother to my kids.

Living Apart—but Staying Engaged

In an early chapter we looked at some of the negative myths and assumptions about women who live apart from their children. Most false notions are focused on what such women could not give to their children—what, in fact, they were taking away from them. But, as we have seen, the reality is that this situation can contain many positive aspects—for the mothers, for the fathers, and for the children as well.

Most of the women we interviewed stayed engaged with their children in a loving, caring way even though they no longer lived with them full-time. They saw their children regularly, took an active interest in their welfare, enjoyed the time they spent together, and guarded it jealously. One of their frequent complaints, in fact, had to do with any efforts by their ex-husbands to reduce their participation in their children's lives. These were what they railed against, not demands that they do more. Far from being "runaway mothers," these women maintained strong connections with their children.

Many women felt that these connections grew even stronger once they and their children were living apart. They felt that they were able to be more loving, more caring, more interested in their children than they had been when they all resided beneath the same roof. This was particularly true of women who had been single parents for a time and found that situation an emotional, physical, and financial strain. When those pressures were removed, these women felt that their relationships with their children improved dramatically.

More to Give

Other women cited the newfound sense of having more to give to their children once they were feeling better about themselves. Released from unhappy marriages, pursuing meaningful work, looking after their own needs, they felt that there was, literally, more to them and, as a consequence, more to give. Their children became the beneficiaries.

> *I know my capacity for mothering has increased a thousandfold. I've given so much to myself that I've come to understand much more*

about giving and receiving. What I did when I got married was to put myself on hold, and eventually I began to feel the consequences of being on hold and so did my children, I'm sure.

There's a resentment that sets in if you tailor your life exclusively to meet someone else's needs, to meet your children's needs. And if that resentment becomes intense enough, then it's difficult to attend to the children. Ignoring your own needs isn't beneficial to the kids, even if you are trying to be the best mother possible. It doesn't matter how hard you try, it's not going to work. To really be able to take care of someone else, you have to build up your own self-esteem. You're no good to anyone without that. So you can have the intention of being the best mother in the world and intend to put your children's needs first but if you're unhappy or unfulfilled or neglecting your own needs, it won't serve the kids. It will backfire.

It's quite easy to see how having additional time and freedom can benefit a woman. Released from the strictures of full-time motherhood, she is now able to pursue her own ambitions, whatever they may be, a freedom men have always enjoyed. For some women this meant establishing a career or continuing or resuming one. For some it meant going to school to train for a career. For others it meant simply being on their own for the first time in their lives and beginning to define themselves to themselves, apart from the framework of a prescribed role. For all of them it meant that they achieved within themselves new levels of self-awareness and self-esteem. They also gained great emotional satisfaction from experiencing themselves as competent people engaged in the world outside of the home. And, for most of them, this new time and freedom allowed them to establish a kind of independent economic stability as well.

I stayed home and raised my kids to a certain age while my husband was free to concentrate on work and to establish himself in his career without the demands of child-care responsibilities being put on him. When we divorced it seemed right to me that I should have the same chance to establish myself. I wanted to be economically self-sufficient and to have work that I really cared about, and I wanted the time to be able to get those things underway. Those didn't seem to me to be outrageous demands.

But one of the main points that many women made about their own search for satisfaction was that they felt they were better mothers at the end of it than they had been before it began. And this was true even though in the latter instance they lived with their children and in the former, they did not. They felt that, far from impoverishing their relationships with their children, the new living arrangements and the new lives they were leading were enriching.

I loved my children. I really did. And there were many things about being a mother that I loved also. But when I was in that marriage there was a whole part of me that was missing, a part of me that was just being squelched. And my dissatisfaction with that state of affairs was growing and starting to push aside even those parts of being a mother that I really did enjoy. That wasn't going to get any better as long as I stayed in the situation. It could only get worse.

The time I spend with my kids now is really remarkable, and I don't think we could ever have experienced this if I'd stayed put, physically or psychically. I'm a much more complete human being now, and I think that reflects in my relationship to my children. It's become richer than it was. That may seem like a contradiction, but the last few years we were living together I was just going through the motions. I wasn't really seeing *them in the way I do now. And my feeling is that I wasn't really there for them to* see. *That's changed completely.*

Now when I'm with them I'm really there, one hundred percent, and I'm sure they feel that. My daughter said to me the other day, "You know, Mom, you're a lot more interesting than you used to be." That made me feel great.

Several women noted that the choice they had made could serve as a powerful example to their children, most especially to their daughters. Their children have seen their mothers, and their fathers, exercising options beyond the obvious ones. They have seen that the traditional modes of behavior are not the only, nor even necessarily the best, ones. They will know that it is possible for a woman to step outside of her designated role and that she needn't be a freak to do so. They will, perhaps, become part of breaking the chain of old myths and assumptions. Their sense of what is possible for both men and women is bound to be different.

> *I feel that my gift to my kids is showing them that change is always possible, that you don't have to be locked into something that's wrong for you. They won't grow up feeling that everything is written in stone. They'll see that life can be a lot more fluid than that.*

More to Take

The other side of the coin, of course, is the children's life with their father. While many of the women we interviewed had differences of opinion with their ex-husbands over one or another aspect of child-rearing, most felt that their children were being well cared for. Most felt that their children's fathers were good and loving parents. Speaking with both mothers and fathers has confirmed for us that men are perfectly capable of assuming the role of primary caretaker, and those who have done so seem to have found it an invaluable experience.

> *I know the big question is supposed to be whether a man can learn to attend to the emotional needs of a child. But it's just a matter of socialization. Men have tended to be very ambitious in terms of their own jobs and therefore have tended to suppress a whole area of themselves. But certainly they can learn to express their own feelings and be sensitive to the feelings of their children. I think it's purely a matter of growing, and I've felt that it's been very important for me, very rewarding.*
>
> *When I was in graduate school or looking for a job or first teaching, it was a very tense situation and I was totally caught up in that. That was part of the difficulty with my ex-wife. She always wanted me to put more time into the family, and I just couldn't. I just didn't have it to give, and I felt that she didn't really appreciate just how difficult and competitive things were.*
>
> *But now I realize that there are rewards for putting time into the family. It's emotionally very satisfying. And it has changed more*

than just my relationship with my son. I mean I literally know more about the world now because I'm more conscious of other people around me. I believe there was a period of my life when I shut that aspect out. I didn't know what other people were thinking and feeling. I was just focused inward. Now my relationships with people have opened up and deepened. I'm very glad my son came to live with me. It's made my life a lot richer.

Theory and Practice

This father's response to living with his son—and it is not an unusual one—makes it evident that though the child's mother may no longer live with him, he is not doing without nurturing. His mother may be missing from his life on a full-time basis, but the caretaking role isn't. That is still very much present, now in the person of his father.

As elementary as this seems, it is a misunderstanding of just this point that feeds the notion that when a mother leaves her children she leaves them to suffer neglect and deprivation. What in fact she does is to leave the children with another adult who has a blood connection, a love and a concern for the children equal to her own. The only difference is that a mother has had assigned to her a role that says she will automatically know how to deal with these children and a father has had assigned to him a role that says he will not. In practice, as we have seen, those rigid assignments often prove to be very wide of the mark.

Certainly the transition from mother as primary caretaker to father as primary caretaker will be smoother for everyone if the father has always been involved in his children's care. And if men continue their current newfound interest in full-time fatherhood, this will surely be the case more and more often. Child-rearing should be a joint effort of both parents from the outset whether or not those parents are ever going to part. We have heard single fathers describe how gratifying it has been for them to be intimately involved in their children's lives, in the day-to-day struggles and joys. There is no reason why fathers in intact families should not experience this as well.

Perhaps we should note again the extraordinary discrepancy that exists between attitudes toward the single mother and the single father in our society. A single mother is expected to handle her child-care chores unassisted, whether she has one child or five. It is presumed that she will take care of a house, wash, clean, cook. She will work outside the home as well, if she needs to, for a wage that will be about half of what a man in the same position would make. She will not be besieged by offers of aid. Her situation seems part of the natural order of things: she is a mother, she is doing what she has to do to take care of her children, she is minding the house, it is as it should be.

A single father, on the other hand, is applauded before he even lifts a finger. At the moment that he assumes the primary care of his children, he is deemed extraordinary, remarkable, practically a saint. All this just for making a commitment he has yet to carry out. To help him do that there will be no dearth of assistance. He will most likely hire a housekeeper whom he will be able to afford to pay. And to take up any slack, there will be volunteers at the ready—friends, relatives, neighbors, eager helpers all.

Of course we are generalizing and, of course, we are also overstating the matter for the purposes of illustration. But not by all that much. The basic point is well taken: single mothers operate almost single-handedly as they struggle to perform what is a very difficult task: raising children alone. We might do well to offer them some of the support and encouragement that we give so freely to single fathers.

We hope it is now obvious that to say a woman lives apart from her children is not necessarily to describe a negative situation. Nevertheless, the reality is that when a mother is not living with her children, there are certain things she can no longer give to them, the kind of things that pass between people who live together on a daily basis. We have already seen that a mother can certainly maintain a loving, caring involvement with her children even though she no longer resides with them. But how can she do that? What are the specific things that she *can* give to her children?

Consulting the Kids

The first is something that can be offered only in some instances, when a mother and father deem it appropriate, and that is giving the children an opportunity to participate in the decision-making process itself. It is certainly not necessary to include the children in this, but some parents with older children choose to do so. Obviously, with younger children, that would be wholly inappropriate. Just as obviously of course, children should never be put in the position of having to choose between their parents.

> *I thought a lot about the children and their reactions, but I didn't keep them abreast of the situation as I went along. All I was feeling was pain, anxiety, and fear, and I didn't want to impose that on them.*
>
> *I talked to the two older kids about their feelings. I felt it would be best for them to stay with their father, to continue living where they were rather than uprooting them, but I wanted to sound them out on it. I'm glad I gave them that time to think it through and arrive at their own ideas about it rather than just presenting them with a fait accompli. We probably would have ended up with the same arrangement either way, but I think it's good that they felt they were part of the decision.*
>
> *We told our kids what we were considering, and if they had felt strongly that they wanted to be with me I would certainly have listened to that. But they were pretty clear on what they wanted and able to express it, and really we all wanted the same thing.*

Regardless of whether or not the children are included in the decision-making process, once the decision is made it is crucial to give the children a thorough explanation of the changes that are about to take place, to clarify just what the decision means and what it does not mean. This is an extremely difficult moment in the life of a child; nothing can alter that. However, a complete and straightforward explanation can help to lessen the destructive impact.

A mother should explain to her children that she is not going to disappear from their lives. She can give the children her reasons for being the parent who is going to move out of the home. And she can stress that she loves the children just as much as she ever has. They will no longer be living together, but that does not mean that her love will stop. A mother should give her children this reassurance frequently.

This period of time, when the decision has just been made and the mother has yet to move out of the home, is a time of preparing the children for the future. There are many different ways to do this but, the most important thing to recognize is that the children do need to be prepared. If the mother has been the primary caretaker, they should know who will look after them when she is not there. Both practical and emotional questions should be addressed and answered as completely as possible. If their questions can be answered—and all children will have them, however reluctant they may be to ask—their fears will diminish.

Long before I even knew for certain what I was going to do, I began teaching my sons to take care of themselves. I taught them how to cook, how to make bread, granola. I'd deliberately keep myself from doing certain things and put the responsibility on them. I also made sure that they learned to get themselves up in the morning and get their lunches made and get off to school. I was trying to ensure that if I was gone, part of their grief wouldn't be that they were helpless, that they'd lost a person who did things for them. I didn't want that to be part of their loss. And doing that made me feel better. Also we had a part-time housekeeper I trained to take a lot of responsibility. And I also deliberately took professional trips, first for a few days, then gradually longer, to see how it would be for me to be away for a while and to see how they'd do without me.

Once we told the kids what we were going to do, I tried to be as sensitive as possible to their reactions. They weren't always dying to talk about it, but if I felt that they were feeling something I'd ask them about it, and I'd keep after them even if they tried to brush it aside or got mad at me. No child can go through something like this without some pretty strong reactions and fears and questions. I wanted to let them know that all those things were okay, and I also wanted to set their minds at rest about whatever I could.

Few women, unfortunately, are as thorough as these two. Many of the women we interviewed said one of the biggest mistakes they made was in their presentation of their decision to their children. They felt that their explanations were inadequate, their reassurances skimpy. This was a time in their lives, as we noted earlier, when their parenting abilities were at a low ebb. Their focus was most often on their own pain and devastation; their energies were devoted to solving their own problems, making their own adjustments. Their children's needs were not the number-one priority. However, this is a point in the process of divorce at which a mother should take special pains to be aware of those needs and to attempt to meet them. She has made her decision. It is her place to help her children deal with the results of that decision.

Staying in Touch—in Every Way

Another thing a mother can give her children even though she no longer lives with them is geographical proximity. There are, of course, instances in which this is not possible. Sometimes the children and father move and the mother cannot follow. Sometimes the mother's circumstances demand that she relocate and leave the children behind. But when a mother can stay close to her children, assuring them of physical access to her, assuring her of consistent, ongoing contact with them, it is certainly best. When a mother is not committed to doing that, the results can be extremely negative.

I moved to the other side of the country some years ago and really lost touch with my kids. I've written them through the years. I've never forgotten their birthdays or Christmas. But it's never been discussed why they're living there and I'm living here. I think I've been afraid of rocking the boat. Two years ago I suggested that they come to visit me and I'd pay their way. They never answered me. So I really have no idea what they feel about all this. I sent them an article that was in the paper here about me and the Mothers Without Custody group that I'm in, but they never responded. Every once in awhile they will write, but they don't express their feelings. I do know though that to other people they call me by my first name. They don't call me Mom. I don't like that at all.

Even when a mother has a strong interest in her children and is a devoted parent, the relationship with them is bound to suffer if she sees her children only sporadically. She simply will not be capable of the level of involvement she could maintain if she saw them more often. Also, distance from her children tends to jeopardize a mother's position as co-parent.

My kids moved with their father to the West Coast, and I was living in the East. Because I didn't have constant contact with them I wasn't aware of my son's increasing difficulties. Then during a Christmas visit I learned that he wasn't enjoying school. He said he didn't like his teacher, and I began to suspect that maybe some things might be going on at home that were reflected in his attitudes. It's certainly no big deal if a kid doesn't like a teacher one year, but I just thought it might be more than that. So I talked to his father, and he said everything was fine. Up until this time things had gone very well, and I hadn't wanted to intrude on the new family that they had—my kids, my ex-husband, and his new wife.

But when I saw that my son was becoming increasingly unhappy, I began to involve myself more in his care. I stepped in in an effort to be of assistance, to be helpful, but my ex-husband was very defensive about my suggestions for our son. He and his wife saw me suddenly, out of the blue, interfering in their family life. So now I have to deal with their hurt, their anger, their confusion, and their suspicion about what I'm doing. They see me as causing problems, maybe trying to take my son away from them, stirring things up.

My ex-husband said to me, "You're not his mother anymore. I see your role now as grandmother or aunt." I was astounded that he would make such a statement. I was astounded by the fact that he had no awareness of the bond between parent and child. I think part of his need to wipe me out is so that he can say to his new wife, "This is your child. You're his mother now." This gets him off the hook as far as having more children.

It seems clear to me now that if I'd been more involved all along and talking to him regularly about my son's welfare, this attitude would never have evolved. But out of my own hesitancy and guilt and not wanting to intrude on the family and seeing that things seemed to be going well, I didn't feel it was necessary to stay in terribly close contact. As a result, I've had months and months of agony. My son needs different kinds of help than what he has been getting, and as his mother I'm committed to seeing that he gets it, whatever the price to me. I'm totally opposed to geographical separation, but if that happens you have to be an involved parent anyway. Period. You have to find a way to do it.

The preceding is a good example of one of the difficulties that geographical distance can cause. And it also suggests a possible remedy. If it is necessary for a mother to live at some distance from her children, to be unable to see them frequently, she should take pains to establish a time for regular discussion about the children with her ex-husband and have that obligation written into their custody agreement. If that is in writing and if the discussions commence at the time of geographical separation, they will come to seem part of a routine. The notion that they represent interference by the mother will be undercut.

It can be very stressful to stay in touch with one's ex-mate. Contact can trigger painful memories and call up old feelings that we would rather forget. For a mother especially, having taken an unusual and, to some, repugnant step, it can touch off or exacerbate feelings of guilt. So we tend to avoid it. If everything seems to be going well, we don't press ourselves to rock the boat. We would rather keep the accent on the positive.

Both a mother who no longer lives with her children and a father who is raising his kids alone will most likely have some questions about their parenting abilities. Are they doing the right thing? Are the kids responding well? Are the kids in the best place? Both mother and father can be rather defensive about their respective positions. A father whose children are living with him may be eager to reassure their mother, and himself, that everything is going splendidly. To say otherwise, he may feel, would indicate that he is not performing his job well. A mother living apart from her kids may be particularly eager to hear that everything is going well. This reinforces her sense that she made the right choice and that the children are adapting well to it.

Nevertheless, for the welfare of the children, both parents might do well to set aside their own needs in this regard. And the best way to do this would be to schedule detailed, frequent—perhaps monthly—discussions between the parents about their children, which are simply part of the routine process of parenting in a divorced family where one parent is living at some distance from the children. Problems, questions, rough spots come up with all children, including those in intact families. But when the family is intact, the children's difficulties can seem a normal, predictable part of childhood. When the family has split up, the problems often seem to be a reflection of that split, and that is when they become loaded issues between the parents.

However, if the custodial arrangements for geographically separated mothers and children include mandated discussions about how the kids are doing, a lot of that extra baggage can be cast off. The focus can be placed where it ought to be: on the children and their welfare. For a mother who sees her children infrequently, this is crucial to her continuing actively in the role of parent.

Working Together

Maintaining a communicative relationship with the children's father is something a mother can give her children whether she lives nearby or far away. Parents who, whatever the differences between them, manage to work together in matters relating to their children are giving those children something precious. The children see that their mother and father, though not wanting to live with each other, are still reasonable adults who are capable of performing their parenting functions and who continue to love their children.

I feel, despite all the mistakes I've made, that I've really thought about my son as much as I possibly could. I've spent a lot of time in therapy on this. I feel good that I've had integrity in my motives and that throughout all of it I've been well intentioned. I've been able to bracket my own needs and really think about my son's.

Sometimes the way I've dealt with my ex-husband has increased the tension for my son, and when that's happened I've tried to change the way I was dealing with him. It's just crucial to keep the child's needs in mind, and the saving grace in this entire thing is that I do believe that his father holds our son's best interests at heart, as do I.

Children lose a lot when there's a divorce. I don't think any of us who didn't go through that as kids can even imagine what that loss is like for a child. You can't add to that the feeling that this child is now just something to be fought over by his parents, just a killing ground where they meet to fight. It's really imperative for a kid to see that his parents can cooperate in dealing with him. I'm not saying that mitigates the sense of loss. I'm just saying that it doesn't add to it.

Children who are forced to observe their parents behaving toward each other like members of opposing armies, battling on every issue, denigrating each other at every opportunity, acting out their own needs for vengeance and retribution, oblivious to the needs of their children, will be bound to feel a greater loss at the time of divorce. Not only has their family been taken from them but their parents, as parents, seem to have vanished as well. As adults, they have become like children, unable to respond to any needs but their own, unable to offer any sense of stability and continuity in a time of upheaval and change.

In addition to the sheer disruption and tension that it causes in children to see their parents going at each other at every turn, it also causes damage to the children's sense of themselves. Children feel strongly that they are part of their parents, their parents are part of them. To hear one parent disparage the other is, for the children, to hear themselves disparaged as well. *If he's rotten, I must be, too. If she's terrible, so am I.* At a time when children are feeling particularly fragile and need all the help and support and reassurance about themselves that they can get, this sort of parental behavior is extremely destructive.

Offering Emotional Commitment

Something else that a mother living apart from her children can offer them is emotional access. We have stressed how important it is to assure the children of physical access, whenever possible. Emotional access is certainly just as vital. Evidencing a high level of involvement is one part of being emotionally available to one's children. Showing an ongoing interest, reassuring the children that she intends to continue in her parental role, are necessary parts of the foundation any mother must lay if she wants her children to feel she is emotionally accessible.

The harder part of guaranteeing emotional access is listening to the children's feelings, whether or not they are pleasant to hear. This is something many women tend to avoid. Burdened already by their own doubts about the course they have chosen, guilty for stepping outside the traditional boundaries of their role, these women fear that hearing their children express feelings of rage and loss and betrayal will be the final blow. They fear they would find hearing these negative feelings unbearable, and they shy away from situations that might lead to such an outpouring. They do not make concerted efforts to elicit those feelings from their children. Just as avoidance and denial can become habitual in discussions between ex-husbands and wives, so these same defenses can come between a mother and her children.

This is another area, however, where it is important to remember who is the child, who the adult—to recognize a parental responsibility, to allow one's own needs to take second place to the needs of one's children. Women who are able to do this find that the rewards are great, for their children as well as for themselves. What seems too threatening—being on the receiving end of a barrage of hostile feelings—can instead become an instrument for liberation.

For it is here that a mother can truly back up her words of reassurance with deeds. She has said that she loves her children, even though she no longer lives with them. She has asserted that the change in their lives is in living arrangements, not emotional commitments. She is still their mother; she intends to continue in that role. Listening to her children's feelings is one way she can demonstrate this. This is her chance to prove that she really means what she says: that she is not going away, that she is not abandoning them, that her parenting has not ended—no matter what the children feel. Her love for them is not conditional; it is not contingent upon their acceptance of her and her decisions.

We do not mean to suggest that this will be easy for any mother. Even women who are certain they have made the right choice for themselves and for their children will find it very difficult to listen to an unexpurgated expression of their children's pain. Those who are more ambivalent about their own course of action will find it excruciating. It is essential, however, to allow this to happen if mother and child are to reestablish a sense of trust. Women who are able to give their children this outlet will find that they have also given something invaluable to themselves.

We find in the course of our work with these mothers that women who were able to make the maximum amount of room for their children's needs in the midst of this difficult and painful process invariably emerged from it feeling more positive about themselves than those who were unable to do so. These latter women tended to withdraw from their children, whereas the former were able to endure the difficult aftermath of the separation and to offer their children support and understanding and constancy through it. These women, it seemed, ended up with connections to their children that were as strong as they had ever been, in some instances perhaps even stronger.

My daughter was enormously angry at me. Why wouldn't she be? I was leaving her—at least that's how she saw it. And I came to realize that the important thing was how she saw it, not my idea of it, not her father's but hers. And I could see that all my protestations of love were falling on deaf ears. It was hard, God, it was hard. There were times when I dreaded seeing her because I knew what it would be like. She treated me as a traitor—that's what I was to her. So I let her act that out without judging her, without raging back at her, which I sometimes felt like doing, and I just kept coming back and coming back and coming back.

In making the choice I had I was asking for time for myself, room for myself, and I felt obligated to give the same to her. She deserved to have room for her reaction. Eventually she saw that she wasn't going to drive me away, and little by little she began to hear what I was saying and to believe that I meant it: that I loved her, that I loved being her mother, that she was precious to me.

I remember trying to get my kids to talk, but they wouldn't for a while. I'd tell them I knew they had feelings they weren't expressing, and it was okay to go ahead and express them. And they'd say, "Oh, Mother!" and then quickly change the subject. But I'd keep bringing it up, and once they did start to talk I almost wished I'd kept my mouth shut. It wasn't easy to hear what they had to say. Sometimes I felt like running out of the room. But of course I didn't, and I'm glad now that I pushed them. They say they're glad too, even though it made them so mad every time I asked them.

When my son was ten years old he decided he wanted to live with his dad. I felt very hurt by that, but I also knew that I had to get past it. He and I maintained a pretty good relationship, I think. We were living nearly a country apart, but I wrote and sent him Polaroid pictures each week. We called each other. I saw him whenever possible. We kept talking to each other. He had made the decision, but he was a little boy.

I've talked to mothers who were angry with their children for making such a choice, but I felt that that just wasn't appropriate. He made the choice he needed to make at that time, and I just worked on keeping the doors open with him. I like him. He's my son. I love him too. I just wanted to have the best possible relationship we could. So he chose his father. Well, that hurt, but that's the way it was. I was just interested in seeing what he and I could build between us in existing circumstances.

I recently remarried—a man who has a fifteen-year-old son who lives with us, a boy the same age as my son, and when my son came to visit us he saw a household with two adults and another kid his own age, and it looked good to him and he decided he wanted to live with us. I'm hoping he'll want to stay, but there are no guarantees. When I knew he was struggling with this decision I wanted to say to him, "You should live with me."

What I did *say was that he had to make up his own mind, that he had to decide what would work out best for him. He recognizes that I didn't pressure him. He also knew that I wanted him. But I told him that he wasn't responsible for his parents' happiness. My feeling is that if you go through something bad you can salvage something out of it if you act honorably and don't put your trips on other people. Then you come out with your self-respect intact. You can feel that you did the right thing.*

Self-fulfilling Prophecy

As we have noted again and again, noncustodial mothers who have no models to follow suffer from the I-must-be-the-only-one syndrome, a guaranteed guilt-producer. But what a woman in this situation can give to her children is a refusal to let that guilt drive a wedge between them, for so often that is the beginning of a terrible cycle that continues to feed itself by creating more guilt. To wipe out this guilt entirely we would have to recast societal attitudes, undo all our conditioning, erase all the myths and assumptions that attach themselves to women who do not live with their children. For as long as those conditions exist, there will be women who internalize them. It is possible to make a start on the job of changing attitudes, but it certainly is not possible to think that it will be completed anytime soon. So it is important for each individual woman to recognize that, while she may suffer some guilt upon making this choice, she need not become its victim.

Perhaps no emotion is more destructive to the relationship between a separated mother and child than guilt. If it is allowed a significant toehold it can truly destroy the relationship.

At the time I left, my son was two and a half, and I felt very confused and overwhelmed. I didn't have the financial resources to set up a viable household, and I felt guilty about that. Also there was a part of me that just didn't want to leave, and that made me even more guilty. I really didn't know what I was doing.

Once I left, my ex-husband never made anything easy for me. Visits were always a fight. And I began to feel that I couldn't see my son regularly, that it was only upsetting him and upsetting me. His father was then living with a woman who had a child the same age as my son, and supposedly the whole household was upset every time my son got to go someplace with me and the other child didn't. It was also very hard for me when the time came to say good-bye. I wanted my son to be part of my life, but I didn't know how to take the responsibility for that.

I've always felt that I was a disruptive, intrusive force in my son's life and that I was looking after my needs and not his. The first few years I tried to see him regularly, but then I just gave up. I decided it would be better for him if I didn't see him. For a number of years I saw him only occasionally. I feel like I abandoned him, and I'm afraid he'll judge me for that.

I've judged myself very severely, as a woman and as a mother. I felt that since I lost my husband and sort of lost my son in the process that I wasn't much of a woman. I feel that I've lost a part of me. I've lost the experience of bringing him up, of him loving me and me loving him, and I still feel guilty about it. This is true even though I know I made the right decision at the time. His father certainly gave him lots of things I couldn't.

And now when I see him it brings up all the pain and all the guilt. I feel guilty about what I'm not, about what I can't give. I feel bad in a very basic way, and I can't believe that I still don't have certain things to give him.

Most women who live apart from their children in no sense abandon them. Yet when such great guilt is present and then allowed to flourish, as it certainly does in the instance just cited, it almost seems to create a self-fulfilling prophecy: I feel I have abandoned my child, ergo I must abandon him. If this mother had not allowed her guilt, and her inability to tolerate it, to push her away from her child, she might by this time have moved far beyond it and be enjoying a satisfying relationship with her son. Instead, she remains mired in it. If anything, her guilt has grown over the years, years in which she was absent from her son's life because she felt that it was too painful for her to be present. She let her guilt come between her and her child, and the cycle continues even today.

But what if all those years ago she had been able to recognize that she could possess certain feelings but that she did not have to act on them? What if she had been able to keep her guilt from becoming the ruling principle of her life? What if, in spite of her guilty feelings, she had *behaved* differently? If she had remained in contact with her son, been involved in his life, demonstrating her caring on a consistent basis, the guilt would gradually have diminished. She would have been able to give to him and to herself. And a good part of her ability to give would have been based on the fact that she had maintained close, consistent contact with her child no matter how guilty she felt. Nothing would have bolstered her self-esteem more than the simple act of not giving up on the relationship between her and her child. Nothing was more damaging to her idea of her own worth than her abdication.

The Quality-time Concept

All the positive things a mother can give her children are the components that go to make up "quality time" between a mother and child. This quality time versus quantity time argument is often cited by women who do not see their children on a daily basis anymore but who maintain that the time they do spend with them is better than it ever was. More fulfilled themselves, more emotionally whole, they are psychically present when they are with their children, something that could not always be said about the period when they lived together daily.

This is a perfectly good argument, and in some instances it may be absolutely true. However, it is also an argument about which it is easy to become glib. Quality time does not just mean time we spend with our children free of the tensions of a disintegrating marriage; or time untainted by our own dissatisfactions about roles and goals; or time that is unmarked by the strains that inevitably occur between people who live together day in and day out. Quality time is a concept that requires a commitment to learning a whole new role, that of visiting parent. We have to reassess our place in our children's lives and acknowledge what things we can no longer do for them and what things we can. Having determined what those things are, we must set about achieving them, even if they sometimes come into conflict with our own needs and desires. And all of this requires a great deal of dedication and love and energy and hard work.

When we look at the women who have successfully made the commitment to part-time motherhood, they bear no resemblance at all to those mythical monster mothers we examined at the beginning of this book. They are not heartless, irresponsible outlaws. They are thoughtful, devoted parents, every bit as determined to do what is right for their children as mothers who live with their kids full-time.

And the fathers we talked with did not fit the stereotype either. They were not unemotional, insensitive nonnurturers. On the contrary, they were quite passionate about their parenthood, grateful for the way in which it enhanced their lives, eager to repay their children in kind.

The Need to Stop Hiding

In light of these success stories, the idea of a woman's living apart from her children seems a perfectly valid option, a reasonable choice rather than a devastating betrayal. It is important that these models become more visible. Women who are considering this choice need to see that it can be made in a responsible, straightforward way. They need to see that it is not necessary to contrive, unconsciously, to "lose" their children via the courts, a threatening ex-husband, poor legal advice, freakish circumstances, or bad luck and then forever after carry the inner stigma of victimization. They need to be given permission to own up to their own needs and desires and to learn that they can acknowledge these and pursue them without abandoning motherhood altogether. They need to learn that an honest evaluation of these needs and desires can in fact be the first step toward making themselves more satisfactory and satisfied parents. They need to stop hiding from themselves.

Our kids were twelve and thirteen years old when we split up after being married fourteen years. At the time we decided to actually make the break my son said, "Mom, I really love you, but I want to stay with Dad." My daughter went with me at first, although she still kept a room in her father's house. I moved with her to an apartment in another part of the city, and I started dating and loosening up and became sort of a hippie, a flower child. It was a very emotional time for me.

I'd gotten married to the first man I ever slept with before I finished college, and I'd never been on my own. I'd never experienced any kind of sexual freedom. So when I was set free I was like an adolescent, and that was difficult for my daughter, I know. I saw her as more of a rival than as my child. I was jealous of her although our love bond was very strong.

In the spring of that first year I decided to take a trip to New York with a friend, and my daughter went to stay with her dad. That was the first time I'd ever gone anywhere by myself. I just fell in love with the city and totally flipped out. I called home and quit my job, and I called my ex-husband and said I'd be traveling for a while and I didn't know how long I'd be away. I was just beginning to experience a kind of freedom. I didn't speak with my daughter when I called. I just told her father I didn't know when I'd be back.

What happened was that he took the opportunity to move her out of the apartment where she'd been with me. He had always wanted her to be with him. I see quite clearly now that he just used that situation to get her there. She would never have left me even though we were having a hard time.

When I got back after my trip I just let it be. I never fought him in any way. I was afraid of him. I allowed my daughter to stay with her father, and that's something I don't really forgive myself for. I'd met a man who made me feel so valued, so loved for the first time in my life, and I didn't really communicate with my daughter at this time. We didn't really talk. It's amazing but a lot of this is just a big blank. I remember my son going out with us but not my daughter.

After six months I broke up with this man, and my ex-husband remarried an old friend of ours, and the kids liked her very much. I was happy about that, but here was this family and I wanted to be part of it, but I couldn't be. I felt the kids were in love with this woman who had come to save their father, and it was really hard. All my life I'd done everything for them, and now they were falling all over this woman. At the same time I was mourning the loss of my daughter. I knew I had to get out of there. I had to make a break.

I went to London on a forty-five-day excursion ticket, and I stayed for a year. A friend told me to write the children often just to tell them that I loved them, and I did that. And they came through London and stayed with me when their father was taking them on a trip to Europe. Then I moved to the West Coast for three years, and I wasn't too far from them. And whenever they wanted to see me I found the money even though that was difficult because I was starting all over again, doing these teenage jobs, like waitressing. And then a few years ago I moved to the East, and they're still out West.

I've lived so many places, and I think my kids feel a desire for me to find a place, a place where they could come and be. But they wouldn't of course because they're grown now. I was always afraid their allegiance to this stepmother would interfere with our relationship, but they constantly reassured me that no one else could take my place because I was their mom. The sad thing is that I loved being with kids all my life, and yet I missed out on my own children's teenage years.

My two sons lived with me for two years after our divorce, and during that whole time my ex-husband kept pressuring me to give them to him. It was very hard having them. I had no alimony and only twenty dollars a week child support. And the kids were giving me a hard time. The only respite I had was once a week when he'd come to take them for the day. I really looked forward to that and to having some time to myself. Well, he kept threatening to take off, to move away, which meant he wouldn't even be there one day a week. Finally I gave in to his pressure, and they went to live with him. They've been with him the last ten years.

I was in a lot of turmoil and conflict at the time, and I really did this without a lot of thought, and it was probably a big mistake. Once the kids were living with my ex-husband he wouldn't cooperate with me, and there were always hassles about visits. Also, I was just in so much pain. I would be terribly anxious before I'd see them, and when they left I'd be just devastated. I always felt when they were with me that they wanted to leave. I always feared that they would turn on me and reject me at some point.

There have been periods over the years when I haven't seen much of them. When I was involved in a relationship I didn't see them too often. I wanted my weekends with my boyfriend. I was very selfish during that time. And then after a while I moved away, and it wasn't so easy to see them frequently. But I've had severe regrets at being left out of their lives.

I feel like an outsider. I've seen many psychiatrists over the years, but it's never been very helpful because I talk about everything but what I need to talk about. One of them told me that I behaved with my kids as if I were their aunt, not their mother. And that was true, I guess. I didn't know what I could give them aside from taking them out to dinners and to the movies and buying them things.

What comes through in these stories is a lack of self-awareness, a lack of understanding by both of these women of the part they themselves played in missing out on time with their children. They felt that they had had their children taken from them against their will, despite some fairly strong evidence to the contrary. In the former instance, the woman was enjoying her newfound freedom, her second adolescence, and saw her daughter as a threat to that. She went traveling in open-ended fashion, not certain when she would return, and made no effort to communicate with her daughter about their living arrangements once she did return. In the latter instance, the woman expressed how difficult it was to take care of her children alone with meager financial resources and a break only once a week.

The pattern in these two cases and in others like them is familiar. Despite the evidence that they might prefer to be on their own, these women cling to their sense of having been victimized, of having been subjected to something beyond their control. Their low self-esteem sinks even lower. As this becomes increasingly uncomfortable, they remove themselves from the situation that is causing them so much pain. They see their children less and less often, and this makes them feel even more inadequate as mothers. Feelings of loss and grief and low self-worth continue, each helping to perpetuate the other.

What these women do not see is that they are the ones who robbed themselves of their motherhood, not by the act of living apart from their children but by refusing to inhabit the role of mother. Their conception of the role-player was of someone who lives with her children and takes care of them daily. When they no longer fit that definition, they felt they had no claim to the role.

Self-victimization

We have seen that a mother's role does alter in some ways when she no longer lives with her children. But we have also seen that in some crucial ways it remains the same. The love, concern, and interest can certainly be constant. However, some women who are dissatisfied with full-time motherhood, but unable to acknowledge that directly, insist upon tossing aside all meaningful involvement with their children and then blame someone, or something, else for their sense of deprivation. Unable to take the responsibility for their own feelings, they seem unable to sustain mature emotional connections with their children. If their own needs and desires did not seem so objectionable, if they were free of the necessity to conceal these, even from themselves, perhaps the results would be different.

The current trend among women to wait to have their children until they are older and more well established may help to alleviate this. The women who fall into the victimization syndrome we have described are generally women who married young and had children right away. They had very little life experience beyond what the roles of wife and mother offered them. They tended to define themselves completely according to the characteristics of those roles. When their marriages broke up, it was unthinkable to them suddenly to define themselves in other terms. They had no idea what those other terms would be. So they clung to the framework of the mother role even as they maneuvered to get free of it. When the maneuvering paid off, however, they felt bereft, stripped, utterly lost.

A woman who waits to have children until she is in her thirties, say—increasingly common today—would be unlikely to experience what we have just described. She would have spent at least a decade of her adult life developing and defining herself as an individual. Without the restrictions of the prescribed role of mother, she would have been free to discover what she liked, wanted, and needed and what she did not. She would know herself as an adult used to operating in the world. She would have had a chance to develop a strong sense of self. This woman, confronting the possibility of living apart from her children, would more likely be able to determine her own needs and acknowledge them. At the same time, she would be less likely to let those needs render her incapable of attending to her children's needs.

Flexibility Is Important

Custody agreements are not written in stone. It is important to know that they can be changed and, in some instances, that they should be changed. It is unrealistic for parents to assume that once they have decided where the children should reside that that decision will be irrevocable for all time. The best solution at one time may not be best at another. Even if everything else remained the same, which is unlikely, the children grow and change, and that alone can dictate revisions in living arrangements.

It is important, for instance, for a parent to be sensitive to the extreme delicacy of the needs of the very young child. Up until the age of two, a child tends to bond strongly with the primary caretaker, and it can be traumatic to have that process interrupted. We would advocate strongly that if the mother has been the primary caretaker, it would be best for her not to separate from the child until she or he is at least two years old. If the father has been the primary caretaker, the same would be true for him. But a child's needs are different from year to year. A good arrangement for a child of three may not suit that same child when she or he is ten or eleven.

Parental needs change as well. A woman who is in school and working and who feels that the children will receive better daily care in their father's household may see things quite differently once she has completed her schooling and established herself in a regular job. It is important to stay flexible, to reassess the circumstances of both children and parents when that seems necessary. One thing that might facilitate that flexibility is writing into the original agreement that the children's residence can be reviewed at the request of either parent.

Counseling Helps

Under even the best circumstances, deciding to live apart from one's children is an extremely difficult choice to make. We did find, however, that those women who received some sort of professional counseling during the period of their decision-making seemed to emerge from that period with more balance and clarity than those who did not. Given a neutral forum in which to air their feelings, they came to understand and accept them more fully than they might have without such support. By virtue of the impartiality of this forum, they were also able to examine their motives more thoroughly and to come to terms with them.

The conflicts a woman experiences in the midst of this process are enormous. Therapeutic support can be exceedingly helpful to her in both understanding and attempting to resolve those conflicts. We should also note that the children of these women will benefit as well. A woman who is getting help and support for herself will be more likely to extend those same commodities to her children.

> *I don't think there's any way I could have gotten through this without therapy. Well, that's not true. I would have* gotten through *but probably not much more than that. I had a place where I could go and vent and rage and question and act out so I didn't have to do any of that with my kids. And I was really able to stick with them and allow them to vent and rage and act out, which is the way it should be. Then I could go back to therapy and deal with how much that hurt, but I didn't have to withdraw from them.*
>
> *I recently met a woman who'd left her kids in Oregon and come East, and we started talking and she described to me how awful it was for her to see her kids after she'd left the house. They were angry and she was miserable, and she said she just couldn't stand it and finally she left. I don't know if I would ever have done that, but I might have withdrawn considerably if I hadn't had some place to go where I could deal with everything I was feeling and also if I hadn't had someone reminding me that I had caused my children this pain and I had an obligation to let them express it to me.*
>
> *Being in therapy during that time really helped me to know what I was doing and, just as important—maybe more important—what I wasn't doing. What I was doing was arranging for the children to be cared for on a daily basis by their father, who loved them and wanted them with him, while I took some steps that would be emotionally and financially important for me. I was also arranging my time so that I would see them at some point every week. What I was not doing was deserting or abandoning them or ceasing to be their mother.*

Obviously, the option we have explored in the course of this book is not for everyone. Many women, whatever the other demands in their lives, would always prefer to reside with their children. Many men would never be comfortable in the position of primary caretaker. But there are other women and men for whom this option seems just right. It offers them an opportunity to step outside of their prescribed roles and explore new parts of themselves. In the process of that exploration some women discover that they are better suited to the role of part-time parent.

> *It was absolutely the right thing for me to do. There were plenty of times when I doubted that, but not anymore. I feel I've grown up in ways that I never could have if I'd stayed in my marriage and stayed with my kids. It may seem like a contradiction, but I know I'm a much better mother today than I was when I was living with them. I have more to give them.*
>
> *The difference today is that I can think of them in a kind of focused, uncluttered way that I never could when I was dissatisfied with myself. Now I can really take them on their own terms and delight in them and see them for who they are. By the end of my marriage, I'd started lumping them together as "the kids" and seeing them as some sort of stumbling block to me. They felt like the force that was holding me back. Today they thrill me. There's no other word for it. And I think I do the same for them. I think they're just as proud of me as I am of them.*

Some men find full-time parenting more fulfilling than anything they have ever done in their lives.

> *I can't think of a single disadvantage to having my son live with me. It only enhances my life. It certainly doesn't take anything away from it. I'm his father. I love that role. I love him. He loves me. It's a real two-way street. Anything I give, I also get back. When my wife and I separated, I knew I wanted my son. I knew I wasn't going to part with him. But I didn't really have any idea how satisfying it would be to share my life with him. That came as a complete and wonderful surprise.*

When this option is the right one for the women and men exercising it, it seems to allow everyone involved to flourish in a most healthy way.

> *I was never happy just being home with the kids. I was never comfortable with that. I just wasn't happy not doing more with my-*

self. But at the end of my marriage I had some therapy, and that helped tremendously in getting me in touch with what I wanted.

There was a tacit agreement in our marriage that both of us would do very stereotyped things. But then as the marriage started falling apart, we started questioning those things. I don't think I could have survived if I'd kept the kids. I don't think I could have been a good mother at that time. I wasn't well on my way in my profession, and I was angry at the kids because I was scared and I didn't know what my priorities should be.

When we decided that the kids would live with him I was very worried about the reaction, the world reaction, my parents' reaction, and the effect on the kids. But I was also very happy about the possibility, and I felt very secure in my relationship with them. I never felt I'd "lose" them or lose contact with them. I've never felt that I'm watching them from afar or missing out on their life. We have joint custody. I live twenty minutes away from them, and I see them at least twice a week.

Don't misunderstand. There was a lot of terrible pain that went along with the decision—pain and guilt and fear and all the other stuff. My main fear was that my kids would construe this as abandonment, that they'd be hurt by it.

But they've been with their father for six years now, and it's been great. The kids are my best advertisement, and that helps a lot. It's been very helpful with my parents. They look at the kids and it's hard to find fault with the decision. They're both very happy, doing very well in school, and they have a certain glow and joy in life, which I like seeing. And I also like how I feel about myself. I like being more in control of what I do. And my husband has become much more of a parent than he ever was.

"Who Will Be Living with the Children?"

A few years ago an article appeared first in the *New York Times* and then in syndication around the country, explaining that we were holding a workshop for women who had elected to live apart from their children. The response we received was extraordinary, not just in its volume but in its substance and its intensity. The two of us had been through this process, and we were well acquainted with the anguish and sense of isolation that can accompany it. Even so, we were astonished by the degree of desperation and loneliness that so many respondents exhibited. Some were women who had already made the choice to live apart from their children, each one certain that she was the only mother who had ever done so. Others were women who had thought about this course but dismissed it as impossible even to discuss, let alone to follow.

It is our hope that this book will help to relieve the aloneness of those women who have made this choice and struggled on their own to deal with the guilt and desolation it so often produces. It is our hope that this book will give courage to those women who entertain thoughts of such a choice but are too ashamed and too fearful to let those thoughts ever move beyond the realm of fantasy. And it is our hope that this book might help both women and men to develop a broader perspective on the whole issue of custody, to realize that the option we have described is one worth considering on its own merits, free of the damaging myths and assumptions that have surrounded it for so long.

You know, I have this fantasy that there will be a time in the future when it is a perfectly acceptable possibility for a woman to do this. I don't know exactly when that will be, but I can imagine it being just as ridiculous to argue over this as it would be today to debate women's right to vote. My fantasy is that a couple is getting divorced and one of the completely natural, almost casual responses to that is to ask, "Oh, who will be living with the children?"

Index

M

N

W